ASPECTS
of SPANISH-AMERICAN
LITERATURE

University of Washington Press
Seattle · 1963

ARTURO TORRES-RÍOSECO

ASPECTS
of SPANISH-AMERICAN
LITERATURE

*

This book is published with
the assistance of a grant from
the Agnes H. Anderson Research Fund
of the University of Washington.

ACKNOWLEDGMENTS

I wish to acknowledge my debt to Dr. Dorothy Shadi for important suggestions for improving the text and to Professor Hugo Rodríguez-Alcalá for suggesting the publication of these lectures. The lectures were delivered during my term as a Walker-Ames Professor at the University of Washington.

A. T.-R.

Contents

ASPECTS
of SPANISH-AMERICAN
LITERATURE

Humor in Hispanic Literature

THE greatest monument of humor in world literature is Cervantes' *Don Quixote*. The humor of this masterpiece lies in the contrast between the apparent and the real, and in the perception of incongruity in the facts of life. Cervantes was a profound realist, a writer who had a deep understanding of man and social phenomena. His standard of judgment was normal, and he took a critical approach to reality. Cervantes knew that the windmills were only windmills, but Don Quixote thought they were giants; hence the incongruity between reason and imagination.

One day Don Quixote met a group of prisoners condemned to hard labor. He ordered the guards to set them free, because they were being taken "against their will." Cervantes, who had been jailed in Spain and taken captive in Africa, knew what it meant to be a prisoner. He understood the bitter reality of acting against one's will, and his knowledge of reality was the basis of his humor. Reason and humor, then, are congenial companions.

Humor, usually allied with the comic, is a negative act that deprives a person of his aspirations to be worthy, intelligent, courageous, or rich. If humor is only this, as is common in the lowest form of satire, it is cruel and unworthy of art. Thus, a character in a play may be deformed to appear only ridiculous, a poem may coldly and cynically satirize a man, and a caricature may be a work of hatred. There is something lacking in this kind of expression. Superior humor has a strong relation with pathos, with human sympathy. If the artist perceives the ridiculous and simultaneously displays understanding and pity for mankind, we are in the presence of superior humor. Without sympathy, humor becomes mockery and invective. One may conceive, however, of a literary masterpiece in which human sympathy and tenderness may be absent; such is the case of *Candide* by Voltaire. Here we have a perfect satire in which the author pitilessly mocks mankind, but *Candide,* in spite of its vitality and imagination, does not have the warm sentiment of Shakespeare or Cervantes.

Shakespeare and Cervantes are masters of the highest form of humor.

> But man, proud man,
> Dress'd in a little brief authority,

Most ignorant of what he's most assured,
His glassy essence, like an angry ape,
Plays such fantastic tricks before high heaven
As make the angels weep; who, with our spleens,
Would all themselves laugh mortal.

Shakespeare makes us aware of the ridiculous in man—his haughtiness, his vain pretenses—but at the same time we feel the tenderness of the poet who sees man's "glassy essence," the tolerance of the artist who himself weeps with the angels on contemplating "our fantastic tricks before high heaven."

So also with Cervantes. When Don Quixote came to the inn, there stood in the doorway two girls of the sort known as "of the district." Don Quixote thought the inn to be a castle and the merry girls a pair of beauteous damsels. When the two women saw Don Quixote in full armor, they made as if to flee inside. "Do not flee, your Ladyships," said Don Quixote. "You need not fear that any wrong will be done you, for it is not in accordance with the order of knighthood which I profess, to wrong anyone, much less such highborn damsels as your appearance shows you to be."

Never having heard women of their profession called damsels, they were unable to restrain their laughter, at which Don Quixote took offense. "Modesty," he observed, "well becomes those with the dower of beauty, and moreover, laughter that has not good cause is a very foolish thing. But I do not say this to be discourteous or to hurt your feelings; my only desire is to serve you." The damsels then relieved Don Quixote of his armor and asked him if he desired to eat something.

This episode is one of the most beautiful and touching in *Don Quixote*. The author's sense of humor is expressed in the contrast between appearance and reality. By the magic of sympathy and tenderness, however, the apparent becomes the real: the two young prostitutes, on hearing themselves called maidens, first laugh, then become serious, and finally, their maternal instincts awakened, ask Don Quixote if he wants to eat something. It may be that Victor Hugo had read this passage when he wrote: "The mockery of the ideal would be a great defect in Cervantes, but observe that in his smile there is always a tear."

Before beginning a brief discussion of humor in Spanish-American literature, I wish to make a few observations on the matter of expression. One of the best channels for expressing humor is language. Play on words, faulty phrases, lofty style expressing superficial thoughts, foreign words to produce a comic atmosphere, and metaphoric conceits are but a few means used to enhance a humorous expression. A reader with an imperfect knowledge of the language will not be able to enjoy all the humor of a writer using these devices. This language mechanism makes translating humorous works very difficult. I do not believe that anybody could render into Spanish, for example, the witty colloquial style of Mark Twain's *The Celebrated Jumping Frog of Calaveras County*. How could the most expert translator do justice to such a funny, imaginative, capricious style as the following?

"He ketched a frog one day, and took him home, and said he cal'klated to edercate him; and so he never done nothing for three months but set in his backyard and learn that frog to jump. And you bet that he *did* learn him, too. He'd give him a little punch behind, and the next minute you'd see that frog whirling in the air like a doughnut—see him turn one summerset, or may be a couple, if he got a good start, and come down flat-footed and all right, like a cat."

The atmosphere created by such a style is unique. If you translate the paragraph word by word you destroy that atmosphere. If you supply new idioms and colloquialisms you create something that is not in the original.

Now let us look at *Don Quixote* in English translation. My impression is that American readers do not enjoy this great work and often consider it very tedious reading. The fault is not the reader's but the translator's. Most translations of *Don Quixote* are deficient. Thomas Shelton's translation (1612), although now a classic in English, is a literal rendering that fails to interpret the most elementary nuances of expression; John Phillips' version (1687) is a mockery of Cervantes' work; in 1700, a tea merchant of London, Mr. Motteux, and a few other gentlemen of good will and little talent gave a new version of *Don Quixote,* not from the original, but from existing English and French translations. Their work has been re-edited many times in England and America. I quote here the opinion of Bertram Wolfe on this popular translation:

... the wretched but time-hallowed translation of Motteux, who was traducer more than translator, who was too lazy and swift of pen to stop for rhythms and subtle meaning where they eluded his first dip into the inkpot, and who, misconceiving Cervantes as another Rabelais, did not hesitate to change the tenor and mood of the whole work into a gross caricature of itself by keying his extravagant slapstick English to a different conception of the characters. Since he thereby substitutes two rather ridiculous fools of low comedy for Cervantes' two lovable ones of high humor and deep humanity, it is not surprising that so many readers have failed to reach the richer Part II or go much beyond the windmills and the blanket-tossing in Part I.

Another translation of the famous book is that of Charles Jarvis (1742), which, in spite of its mediocrity, has run through one hundred printings; other versions published in England down to 1867 are only revisions of extant translations.

Translations of this kind could not awaken a great enthusiasm for *Don Quixote* in the English-speaking world. By the end of the nineteenth century, however, a group of able translators had begun to work in earnest at the task of revealing the charms of Cervantes' masterpiece. Thus we have the following versions: Duffield's (1881), Watts's (1888), and Ormsby's (1885). The first two are written in archaic style and therefore sound more like Shakespeare than Cervantes; Ormsby's translation avoids all affectation and is in many ways the most successful of all. In our century we have two translations of real merit: one by Robinson Smith (1908), an excellent scholar, and one by Samuel Putnam (1949).[1] Mr. Putnam gives us some interesting data on the art of translating. He has tried to avoid on the one hand an antiquated style and vocabulary and on the other hand any modernism that would be out of place or savor of flippancy. Cervantes, one of the most modern of Spanish writers, stands in no need of modernizing; his Spanish is essentially the Spanish of today, and the thing to do would seem to be to let him alone, to let him speak for himself, while his translator strives for perfect naturalness and shuns all affectation.

The translator himself begins to realize the difficulty—the impossibility—of his task. "To let him alone, to let him speak for himself" means to let him speak in Spanish, not to translate him. The problem appears in the very first words of the book, in the title itself: *El ingenioso Hidalgo don Quijote de la Mancha.* The translation begins, "The Ingenious Gentleman," but, Mr. Putnam adds, " 'ingenious,' needless to say, is not a proper translation of 'ingenioso.' " Smith, in his first edition, gives "imaginative" for "ingenious" and, in his revised edition, "visionary." Mr. Putnam uses "ingenious," and his reasons for so doing are certainly ingenious:

Either "visionary" or "imaginative" is unquestionably closer to the original if one does not take into account the semantic associations; but it seems to me that by this time the word "ingenious" in the sense that the literal-minded Shelton gave it, has so embedded itself in our consciousness as we think of Don Quijote that it would be a mistake to change it on the title page.

We may retort that the word "ingenious" may be embedded in Mr. Putnam's mind, but not in the minds of thousands of readers who will read the book for the first time.

Let us pass to the word "hidalgo," meaning a person of noble class. A gentleman originally was one entitled to bear a coat of arms, but today the meaning is quite different; therefore, Mr. Putnam uses the word in its archaic significance. The word "gentleman" is embedded in our minds in its modern meaning, and it seems to me it would have been better to use the term "knight."

If we have so much trouble translating the title, you may guess the innumerable difficulties that the translator will meet in the text. Mr. Putnam is an excellent translator, and yet his version is far from having, as the cover caption says, the glory and the humor, the meaning and the feeling, of the original.

The language of Don Quixote is organic. The knight has his own vocabulary, his own metaphors, his own subtle fineries of speech. No other Spaniard speaks the way he does. Don Quixote cannot speak in English. The case of Sancho is still more absolute. Sancho's language is so full of twists and turns, proverbs, colorful words, picaresque allusions, maxims, colloquialisms, mistaken locutions, and changes of word meanings that to translate his speech is to betray his personality. Reading the dialogues of Sancho in English gives me the same strange sensation I felt when I heard *Hamlet* played in Portuguese.

Humor, at least in a literary form, seems to be the product of a refined society. The sixteenth century in Latin America was a period of invasion and conquest, a continuous crusade, and a movement of frontiers, both physically and spiritually. Soldiers were brutal and heroic; monks and missionaries were burning with religious passion; historians were immersed in a sea of miraculous monsters or dazzled in a succession of stormy events; poets felt, in the clash of two races, the tragic sense of life and the grandeur of immortal actions. The poets were modern Homers in the presence of one hundred Iliums; they sang epic songs to the new Achilles, Hector, Odysseus, Agamemnon, and Menelaus, whose names if less poetic are no less heroic —Cortés, Alvarado, Pizarro, Valdivia, and Almagro. The century was not propitious for tender lyricism or humorous relief.

Colonial society of the seventeenth century offered a very fertile field for irony and satire. Great wealth, luxury, laziness, sedentary habits, and clandestine love affairs favor the development of erotic poetry and satirical verse. Lima was the center of refinement in the New World and the cradle of wit and humor. Here we find Juan del Valle y Caviedes, the sharpest tongue of this period. Caviedes was the son of a wealthy Spaniard. At the death of his father he devoted himself to copious drinking and multiple love affairs, as a result of which he lost his fortune and contracted syphilis. To regain his fortune he became a peddler. He rented a place in the old plaza of Lima, bought a table, and established a sort of five-and-ten-cent business. To regain his health he turned to medicine; but the doctors could not give him back his health, and he was unable to remake his wealth. Disappointed and embittered, he wrote many satires against women and physicians, which later appeared in his now famous book: *Tooth of Parnasus, Physician's Wars, Medicinal Prowess, Exploits of Ignorance, by Juan Caviedes, a patient miraculously escaped from the mistakes of doctors thanks to the protection of Glorious Saint Rock, guardian saint against physicians or against Pestilence, which is about the same. Its author dedicates this book to Death, Empress of Physicians, to whose glorious reign they present offerings of human lives and pay tributes of health in the form of dead men and patients.*

Caviedes sharply satirized the most important doctors of Lima; he mentioned them by their own names or by their nicknames; he heaped insults and abuse upon them, and in so doing he left to posterity a monument of satire comparable only to that of Quevedo in Spain. His sense of humor derives from his sufferings and from his hatred; it is always bitter and black and never sanguine; it does not, like the humor of Anatole France, sleep "siesta" or wear pajamas and bedroom slippers.

Is humor an attribute of youth? According to Alfonso Reyes[2] humor possesses in mature irony what it lacks in heroic enthusiasm. Humor enjoys laziness and comfort, typical delights of middle age. If one thinks of Chesterton, Oscar Wilde, and Anatole France, one would agree with Reyes. This statement may also be applied to the Mexican writer, Fernández de Lizardi, author of the picaresque novel, *The Itching Parrot,* published in 1816. Lizardi was one of the earliest fighters for Mexican independence. At the beginning of the struggle, Lizardi entered directly into the political arena, but after being jailed for his ideas, he made his literary work an instrument of social criticism, and wrote *The Itching Parrot:*

Periquillo was sent as a gentleman's son to the University, although he had neither an inclination for study nor any real desire to engage in a learned profession. After obtaining the degree of Bachiller, Periquillo cast about for the professon requiring the least amount of preparation. As theology best met his requirement, he began to prepare for the priesthood; but he wasted his time, and evil companions diverted him from his studies. The threat of his father to apprentice him to a trade drove him in desperation to enter a monastery, for anything, he thought, was preferable to tarnishing his honor by engaging in a trade.... The rigorous life held few charms, and his stay within the walls was short. A small inheritance left on the death of his father a few months later was quickly squandered. An escapade followed which led to his imprisonment. His release was obtained by an unscrupulous notary whose only purpose was to secure Periquillo's service as a clerk. After freeing himself from this master, our hero passed from one adventure to another, suffered dire poverty, enjoyed to the fullest such wealth as came through occasional turns of fortune, and, with it all, ran the whole gamut of masters usually found in a picaresque novel. In the end, in contrast to the typical Spanish *pícaro,* he mended his ways and died a respected citizen.[8]

In *The Itching Parrot* the incongruity between appearance and reality is always obvious. The real in this novel is the hidden purpose of Lizardi, his critical and moral attitude; the apparent is Periquillo's false conception of values. The shortcoming of this novel is excessive realism. The adventures of the hero, Periquillo, are not touched by the intuition of the author, and no universal perspective is seen in the individual experience. The essence of the book is the recording of a succession of experiences taken directly from life, for the purpose of ridicule. The success of this satire is due to an exuberance of comic situations rather than to a poetical quality. The comic element appears objectively, in very elementary forms—the joke, the ridiculous situation, the sense of the ludicrous. Nowhere do we see the poetic display of imagination, the deep humanity, that we find in the great classic novel, *Lazarillo de Tormes,* in the case, for instance, of the noble squire who, having been without food for several days, poetically praises the food his servant is eating and finally condescends to taste it.

In *The Itching Parrot* we have facts, brutal reality, slapstick comedy, direct criticism, and a superabundance of detailed observation, but seldom that feeling of sympathy and tenderness always present in *Don Quixote* and in *Lazarillo de Tormes.*

If Lizardi's humor is satirical and sarcastic, that of

Ricardo Palma, a Peruvian writer of the second half of the nineteenth century, is graceful, anecdotic, and sound. It is the expression of a man of good humor, witty and sharp, who is highly responsive to the comic aspects of man and society. Palma is the inventor of a new prose genre called Peruvian traditions. The tradition is a spicy commentary on a historical event, a legend, or a simple fantasy. Palma is so rich in observation that in two or three pages he reveals a character, creates an atmosphere, or unties a historical knot. The *Traditions* constitute a complete picture of the social, religious, and popular history of the Peruvian nation. By way of illustration I give here a résumé of one of his *Traditions,* in which a friar performs one of the many miracles that had given him the reputation of a saint.

A certain peddler in Lima goes to Fray Gómez in search of a five-hundred-dollar loan to develop his business. Fray Gómez asks him how he can imagine that in such a poor cell he would find five hundred dollars. The peddler says, "I have faith that you will not disappoint me." Fray Gómez answers, "Your faith will save you. Wait a moment."

Looking around the cell, Fray Gómez sees a scorpion crawling on the window frame. Wrapping the scorpion in a page torn out of an old book, he tells the peddler: "Take this, my good man, and pawn this little jewel, but don't forget to return it to me in six months."

The peddler goes to a money lender, who is struck by the beauty of the jewel, and offers him two thousand dollars for it. The peddler refuses the offer and insists on accepting no more than five hundred dollars for six months.

The peddler's business goes so well that at the end of the six-month period he recovers the jewel, and he returns it, wrapped in the same paper in which he received it, to Fray Gómez. Fray Gómez takes the scorpion, places it on the window frame, blesses it, and says, "Little creature of God, continue on your way." The scorpion walks away freely on the walls of the cell.

In spite of the harmless irony in this story, the Catholic Church frowned on this kind of humor, and Palma was considered an irreverent writer.

There are, of course, many other humorous writers in the nineteenth century, even in the romantic period, when poets and novelists so exaggerated passion and suffering that the exaggerations became extravagant and comic. The romantic writer lacks common sense to such a degree that many of his ideas, attitudes, and phrases seem ridiculous to us. The Spanish romantic Espronceda, disillusioned in love, decides to die, and ends his poem with the line: "One more cadaver, what matters to the world?" Espronceda also speaks to the sun in these terms: "Stop, oh Sun. I salute you!"

The Mexican poet, Manuel Acuña, before committing suicide, gave us a wonderful picture of happiness, in which appear the beloved woman, the poet, and between the two, his mother like a god—a natural situation in nineteenth-century Latin society, but highly amusing in today's Anglo-Saxon society. The Cuban poet, José María Heredia, on contemplating Niagara Falls, wishes he had a pale beauty fainting in his arms. Innumerable ladies died of love in our romantic novels and plays; their lovers sometimes killed themselves on the ladies' tombs.

Twentieth-century literature is more sophisticated. At random I have taken three humorous writers—a Chilean, a Mexican, and an Argentinean. Let us see how they react in face of the incongruous and the ridiculous.

Genaro Prieto, a Chilean novelist, is the author of *Dead Man of Poor Judgment* and *The Partner,* which has been translated into English.

The Partner is the story of Julián, a man in need of financial help. He goes to his friends in search of a job or a loan, but he always gets the same answer: "I would like to help you, friend, but I have to consult with my partner."

When Julián himself is approached by a former schoolmate with a fantastic financial project, he decides to follow suit, and answers: "Yes, I am interested, but I have to talk to my partner." Since the case is urgent, he has to create a fictitious partner immediately, a man with a solid name and reputation, Mr. Walter Davis.

Julián becomes the junior partner of Mr. Davis and begins to speculate in the stock exchange in a most spectacular manner. Julián's wife is happy because their economic situation improves, but unhappy because her husband is away from home in the company of Mr. Davis. Early in the story Anita falls in love with Julián. The phenomenal successes of Julián put the partner's name in the limelight, and Mr. Davis becomes a spectacular figure, much to Julián's discomfort. Speculators crowd Julián's office and ask him: "What does Mr. Davis think of such and such a stock?" "Could Mr. Davis advise us on this investment?"

When Julián wants to sell his own stock, his brokers demand that he get the indorsement of Mr. Davis. Julián goes to Valparaiso, where Mr. Davis is supposed to live, disguises himself as an Englishman, goes to a notary public and signs a document with Mr. Davis' signature, authorizing Julián to sell the stock. When Julián gives an opinion on the position of the stock market, his friends smile skeptically and say: "This is Mr. Davis' opinion." When Julián remains away from home, usually in Anita's company, his wife gets a beautiful gift from Mr. Davis, apologizing for having kept her husband in conference all night. She is very grateful and urges Julián to invite the Englishman to dinner. Anita herself is very much intrigued by the mysterious Mr. Davis and wishes to meet him.

Julián is so annoyed by this situation that he finally confesses that there is no Mr. Davis, that the whole thing is a fraud. It is too late. Nobody believes him. On the contrary, he is accused of being disloyal to his partner.

Julián is now desperate and decides to put an end to the fantastic partnership. He writes an article in a leading newspaper explaining to the public that since he, Julián, has been the brain of all the transactions of the society, and since Mr. Davis has not acknowledged this fact, he has decided to end the partnership. The next morning he writes Davis' reply, a violent letter against Julián, stating that his partner does not act like a gentleman in dissolving the society.

Julián is now happy. He can prove to his wife, to his mistress Anita, to his brokers, and to his friends that he is a financial genius and that Mr. Davis was only his wealthy partner. With the newspaper in his pocket, he goes to the Club where he meets some friends who reproach him for his indifference to Mr. Davis' attack. Mr. Davis has called his conduct ungentlemanly. What is he going to do about it? A duel is imperative.

Julián is thus forced to fight a duel with a ghost— but what will he do about the seconds? They will have to meet Mr. Davis, and Mr. Davis does not exist. Julián then addresses a letter to himself, signed by Mr. Davis, in which the Englishman challenges him to a duel without witnesses in a forest. Julián rides to the deep recesses of the Andes to meet his enemy. In the darkness of the night the horse is frightened and throws the rider, who hits his head against a tree. Julián has a hallucination: he sees Mr. Davis aiming at him with a revolver. The two men shoot simultaneously and the Englishman is hit. When Julián comes to his senses, he thinks he has killed Mr. Davis. He returns to the city with a feeling of final liberation.

The papers have published a detailed account of

the duel with pictures of both men. Mr. Davis appears as a very handsome Englishman. Anita, who has fallen in love with the mysterious foreigner, calls Julián a murderer; even Julián's wife is very much concerned with Mr. Davis' fate.

Several months go by. Julián continues his financial transactions now without success. In a short time he is completely ruined. It is natural, say his friends, now that there is no Mr. Davis to advise him.

From here on, the book takes a tragic turn. Julián's child dies; Mr. Davis' shadow has killed him. A friend informs Julián that the latter's wife is deceiving him with Mr. Davis. Mr. Davis has been seen visiting his house when Julián was away. Julián quarrels with his wife, and she abandons him. He is left alone. It is late at night. A shadow appears before the bewildered Julián. It is Mr. Davis. Julián shoots at the shadow, but Mr. Davis does not die. "How can I die," he exclaims, "when I am only a creation of your brain?" Julián tries to find a solution to avenge himself on the man who has ruined him, has killed his child, and has taken away his wife. He sits down to write a letter in which Mr. Davis threatens to kill him; then he shoots himself.

The police report is murder. The wound, according to the experts, could not have been self-inflicted; besides, another shot had been fired; finally, Mr. Davis' letter proves everything. The police were never able to apprehend Mr. Davis.

The picaresque novel is probably the most typical expression of Spanish literary genius. It developed in the sixteenth and seventeenth centuries; it produced masterpieces such as *El Lazarillo de Tormes, Guzmán de Alfarache,* and *El Buscón;* it passed into France where Lesage wrote his famous *Gil Blas,* and then into Mexico with Lizardi's novel *The Itching Parrot.* Since then many writers, with little success, have tried this form of novel. One of the last efforts to revive this genre is *The Usless Life of Pito Pérez,* by the Mexican writer Rubén Romero.

A picaresque novel has three basic elements: humor, real observation of life, and pathos. Originally it also had a moralizing purpose, but this element is no longer considered indispensable. If the picaresque novel has no humor, it is only a moral tract; if it is devoid of exact observation, it is not true to life; if it has no pathos, it becomes cruel buffoonery.

In some contemporary works of our continent, such as *Tortilla Flat*—that charming story of the *paisanos* of Monterey—and *The Useless Life of Pito Pérez,* which I consider typical picaresque novels, moralizing hardly appears. I would like to include *Tortilla Flat* in my observations on humor in Spanish-American literature, but for obvious reasons I must not do so.

The Useless Life of Pito Pérez belongs very definitely to the picaresque genre. It tells the story of Pito Pérez, a Mexican hobo, who follows rather closely the example of the rascals of the Spanish picaresque. He is a choir boy, drugstore clerk, counselor to a priest, missionary, and finally a traveling salesman. He relates his life to the author, at the pay rate of a bottle of tequila for each episode. Pito describes his unfortunate love affairs, his adventures in various jails in Mexico, and his sad experiences in several hospitals.

Toward the end of the novel, just before Pito Pérez is found dead on a pile of rubbish, he speaks to the author about his most faithful sweetheart, a woman he stole from the Zamora hospital. She is a woman of much virtue and tenderness, a submissive being who watches day and night over Pito's life, an acme of perfection. The author cannot conceive of a human being so perfect and asks: "Who is she, Pito Pérez? "Who is she?" answers Pito, "The skeleton of a woman that the students of medicine of Zamora used in their anatomical studies."

There is a great deal of humor in this book. Humor is here an act of "devaluation"—it exists in the destruction of the hero's aspirations, in his failure to be; but there is also a good amount of objective humor, observable in the simple fact of the hero's presence. Pito Pérez amuses the reader as a type, a hobo or *peladito,* very much as Cantinflas amuses the Mexican spectator, or Charlie Chaplin the American audience. Besides this "devaluation" of the character, there is another important element: the author's sympathy for his hero, without which there would be no humor.

Pito Pérez is an anarchical philosopher. He does not believe in work; he believes in the Devil rather than in God, in the "poor Devil," hated by everybody;

he does not respect anybody because nobody respects him; he loved but was fooled by his sweethearts; only a skeleton of a woman is worthy of being loved. Therefore, he drinks tequila while others work; he steals from the wealthy as an act of justice; he makes love to his master's wife "just to be obliging." He pities the poor and advises them to respect the law and to spit in the faces of lawmakers and politicians. He is true to his beliefs even after death; when he dies in the dump, the useless ashes of a forgotten man are lost forever, mixed with the dust of the earth.

There are many similarities between Pito Pérez and Charlie Chaplin's characters. Pito is a social critic, a satirist, a man with a social outlook and a deep insight into human nature. Romero and Chaplin use their talent in a humorous and pathetic manner to expose social evils and cankers, leaning with great understanding toward the underprivileged. In both authors we frequently find a combination of satire, pathos, and fantasy. In *One Night Out,* "while being dragged along a path by Ben Turpin, Chaplin suddenly plucks a daisy and smells it. In a moment the drunk is transformed into a poet." Pito Pérez, starving and almost naked, goes up to the church's belfry "to fish out memories with the bait of the landscape." In both authors we detect also a richness of invention, tenderness, and gravity, which goes deep into the universal in human nature. In *A Dog's Life,* for example, Chaplin is a vagabond philosopher who criticizes social conventions and stupidities: "Living is, for the common man, a dog's life, but that is no excuse for not making the best of it." Pito Pérez also lives a wretched life, but he consoles himself with the knowledge that if others enjoy his sufferings and laugh, he must also enjoy them. To be optimistic all he needs is a bottle of brandy.

The resemblance between *The Kid* and *Pito Pérez* is striking. Chaplin exploits the theme of "the little man who lacks material possessions but is a person of position in his own dream world." He is the gentle tramp-philosopher leading a meager existence but dreaming of a better day. Pito Pérez also has his inner world in which "he achieves what society denies him in real life." In *The Circus* and in *City Lights* we find the same humorous and pathetic resources that are used in *Pito Pérez*: the loss of a girl to a happier rival, sentimental scenes fraught with pathos and suffering, and a great penetration into the human soul. Finally, in *Modern Times,* Chaplin seems to be an incarnation of Pito Pérez: "Fleeing from the factory he goes through one adventure after another, each time being robbed of another illusion, until at the very end he faces life in complete uncertainty and helplessness."[4]

The Argentinean writer, Arturo Cancela, may be considered a genuine American humorist. In his book, *Tres relatos porteños,*[5] Cancela presents a picture of Creole psychology and customs, contrasting them with the usual ways of Europeans. The story entitled *Dr.*

Herrlin's Bacillus is already a classic of the genre. It runs as follows.

Dr. Augusto Herrlin, of the University of Uppsala, publishes his report on a new sickness of the rabbit (*Lepus cuniculus vulgaris*). Dr. Herrlin, being only forty, is considered a young man with a great future. He has been engaged to the seventh daughter of Professor Hedenius for the past eight years and therefore dedicates the report to her:

> To my sweetheart
> Harolda Hedenius
> Who, to her virtue and beauty,
> Adds a name illustrious
> In the conquests of microscopic Flora.

It occurs to the Argentinean Consul in Stockholm that the findings of Dr. Herrlin may be very valuable in Argentina, a land afflicted with the rabbit plague. He sends a report to the effect that Professor Herrlin has discovered a bacillus capable of exterminating the wild rabbit. The Minister of Agriculture invites the Swedish scholar to come to Argentina and direct the campaign against the rabbit. He also appoints Dr. Simón Camilo Sánchez to head the new division of "War on the Rabbit." Dr. Sánchez is the ideal man for the job, since he already holds the positions of Director General of Agriculture, Cattle-Raising, and Pisciculture; Professor of International Law; Lecturer on Consular Service and American History; and Instructor of Political Science and Philosophy of Law.

Dr. Sánchez goes to work. In a few days he has created the new Department of Agricultural Protection (the D.P.A.). According to his plans the territory of the republic is divided into twenty zones, each headed by a commissar whose duty it is to inform the Buenos Aires office weekly on rabbit activity. The minister accepts the plan, and with a budget of a half-million dollars and a staff of two hundred and fifty, the D.P.A. begins to function. Its first task is to make a map of the republic showing in blue ink the places infested by the rabbits. The whole surface of the land is blue, as if over the whole Argentinean territory somebody had poured a bottle of Stephens' ink.

The first reports of the D.P.A. state that the rabbits are quadrupeds, mammiferous, very fast, and extremely fertile. The commissar from Mendoza, for so much information, demands one hundred employees, instead of ten. The minister is forced to reorganize the D.P.A., appointing twelve hundred new employees. The Buenos Aires office has to be enlarged with new departments: the personnel office, the office of statistics, and the propaganda section—in short, three hundred new employees. The country is flooded with pamphlets, billboards, signs, and maps of the republic horribly spotted with blue. In the most remote places of Argentina the only rabbits one can see are those of the billboards proudly displaying this inscription: "The rabbit is the worst enemy of Agriculture."

In the midst of this preliminary work, Dr. Herrlin arrives in Buenos Aires. His arrival is most inopportune, since the socialist members of Congress are attacking the $1,500,000 budget demanded by the D.P.A. Since the budget is under fire, the best policy for Dr. Herrlin to follow is to lie low; therefore, when Dr. Herrlin appears at the Ministry of Agriculture, a young secretary asks him to go home for the time being and to remain incognito. Days and months go by, and Dr. Herrlin's only activity is to collect his monthly check and to stroll through the streets of Buenos Aires. Tired of this life, he goes to live at the boardinghouse of Doña Asunción Fragoso, where one night, after copious libations, he makes his first contact with the enemy, a huge rabbit who is Doña Asunción's pet. This rabbit, whose name is Don Pepe, gives the doctor much trouble in the days to come.

While the bacillus is being prepared in the Institute of Bacteriology, the rabbits increase in such proportions that they eat every green thing in the land; the personnel of the D.P.A. increases still more, and they eat out of the public treasury even more than the rabbits eat off the land. The budget reaches the colossal figure of eight million dollars, while the socialists protest, demanding proof of the D.P.A.'s worth in the form of a single rabbit's cadaver.

Finally, the Model Institute of Agricultural Bacteriology is inaugurated. In attendance at the ceremony is the president of the republic. Dr. Herrlin, who makes the main speech, says, among other things, that the rabbit species gave its name to the most chivalric nation in the history of the world, Spain. "Philologists," he says, "maintain that the word 'España' means rabbit, since the Hebrew name of this animal was 'Saphan,' which in Phoenician gave 'Sphania' and in Latin 'Hispania.' "

The morning after the speech Dr. Herrlin is challenged to a duel by a Buenos Aires newspaper director, a red-blooded Spaniard who accuses Dr. Herrlin of having insulted Spain's honor by calling her *"cuniculosa."* Dr. Herrlin refuses to fight and signs a document expressing his love for Spain and declaring that Strabo, Pliny, and Catullus, his historical sources, were all pamphleteers who had created the black legend of Spain. One of the seconds, however, is not satisfied and writes that Dr. Herrlin is a coward who is fighting the enemy from a laboratory room. "We Spaniards," he says, "would kill the rabbits face to face."

Political intrigues are centered now in the new institute. A new junta is created to control Dr. Herrlin's activities. At the head of this organization is Dr. Anibal Gaona, who later on, because of his distinguished work against the rabbits, becomes a candidate for the presidency of the republic. The Socialist party backs the candidacy of Dr. Vertiz, who maintains that the rabbit does not exist but is only an invention of the present government. In the midst of this political fight, the enemies of Dr. Gaona attack the Bacteriological Institute. Dr. Herrlin, hit on the head by a stone, is hospitalized and suffers a case of amnesia. He forgets his Spanish; all his Buenos Aires experiences are erased from his mind, and he remembers only the old days in Uppsala and his dear sweetheart, Harolda.

From the hospital he is sent back to the boardinghouse of Doña Asunción. Doña Asunción takes such excellent care of the doctor that in a few months he begins to remember his life in Argentina and his Spanish, but forgets his Swedish and his old sweetheart in Uppsala. Don Pepe, the rabbit, becomes his closest friend, and one day this poor creature finds a little tube containing the Herrlin bacillus; with the curiosity typical of a rabbit, Don Pepe tastes the liquid from the tube and soon dies in Doña Asunción's arms. The poor lady is deeply affected by this loss. Dr. Herrlin, realizing the great damage he has caused, wishes to console Doña Asunción and so he marries her. Don Pepe is buried in the garden, and over his tomb Dr. Herrlin inscribes: "Here lies Don Pepe, first and only American victim of the Herrlin Bacillus."

Not only do the three contemporary novelists chosen for this paper represent the sense of humor of their respective countries, but each represents a different kind of humor. In Genaro Prieto's work we have a clear example of dramatic irony: the successful life of Julián leads finally to disgrace and death; in *Pito Pérez* we have an excellent example of satire, that is to say, the transcribing, for the purpose of ridicule, of a series of characteristics copied directly from fact; in *Dr. Herrlin's Bacillus* we find an ironic attitude, a capacity to detect the ridiculous in daily life and then to exaggerate it to produce humorous effects.

These three authors are officially considered as "humorists" by literary critics. A complete study of humor in Latin America would presuppose a careful review of all our literary values, a re-evaluation of the whole field of belles-lettres. As the present writer believes that he himself enjoys a good sense of humor, he did not wish to inflict upon you the findings of his critical analysis of three thousand writers.

José Enrique Rodó
and His Idealistic Philosophy

 osé Enrique Rodó was born in 1871 in Montevideo and died in Palermo in 1917. In 1897 he wrote his first essays: *El que vendrá* and *La novela nueva,* in which he shows intense concern about literary Americanism. In 1899 he published his essay on Rubén Darío, a masterpiece of literary criticism; in 1900 he published *Ariel;* and *Liberalismo y Jacobinismo,* an extremely broad-minded interpretation of religion, appeared in 1906. His masterpiece, *Motivos de Proteo,* was published in 1909. His last book, *El mirador de Próspero,* appeared in 1913.

El que vendrá analyzes the Spanish-American background; *Ariel* explores the living conscience of a continent; and *Motivos de Proteo* deeply probes the soul of man. "To renew oneself is to live; it is the law of time and man's destiny; travel is the best way to achieve self-renewal," Rodó wrote. At the peak of his genius, when he was forty-six years old, he undertook his first trip to Paris, which he considered the center of modern culture. He never reached his destination, for he died in Italy.

The story of his life is colorless. Rodó was simply a modest teacher and newspaperman. He was no hero, no lover; he was not even a good orator. His intellectual honesty was recognized and admired by the youth of his country. He was a serene yet forceful thinker, and his thinking had the broad human perspective of the classics. *Ariel* has become his greatest contribution to Latin-American culture.

Rodó wrote *Ariel* before he was thirty years old, but it reveals the discipline, knowledge, and intensity of a mature man. *Ariel* has achieved masterpiece stature through the years. It is the work of a poet, a teacher, a philosopher—a threefold combination that might symbolize the essence of a complete man.

The teacher, Próspero—named after the wizard in *The Tempest*—meets with his students for the last time; a cycle of learning is coming to an end. The students are seated beside a bronze image of Ariel. The symbol is eloquent and clear:

Ariel embodies the mastery of reason and of sentiment over the baser impulses of unreason. He is the generous zeal, the lofty and disinterested motive in action, the spirituality of civilization, and the vivacity and grace of the intelligence; the ideal end to which human selection aspires; that superman in whom has disappeared, under the persistent chisel of life, the last stubborn trace of the Caliban, symbol of sensuality and stupidity.[1]

Próspero's last lecture is a lesson in idealism, in noble motives and lofty ideas, as well as a lesson in optimism; the first duty of a young man is the conquest of his own self. Paraphrasing Renan, Rodó says: "Youth is the discovery of that immense horizon which is life."

The cult of youth was born in Greece. Enthusiasm and hope are "the gifts of the youthful spirit." For this reason Jules Michelet, the French historian, compared the activity of the Greek soul to a happy game, about which are grouped, smiling, all other nations on the earth.[2] The cult of hope and enthusiasm, however, must not lead us to forget doubt and suffering or give us a false sense of security based on ignorance: governments are prone to protect youth from works considered morbid or unhealthy:

No firm training of the intelligence can be based on simple-minded isolation or on voluntary ignorance. Every problem proposed to human thought by the spirit of Doubt, every sincere reproach which is fulminated against Nature or against God himself from the breast of disheartenment or sorrow, has a right to reach our consciousness and there be considered and faced.[3]

Rodó feels that America is in desperate need of her youth, and his strongest desire is to mold the moral orientation of the young. He sees everywhere the danger of human beings isolated in a society dominated by the specialist, chained to the millstone of monotony:

The divergence of individual vocations will impress divers directions upon your activities and cause to predominate in each one of you a disposition of mind predetermined by a definite aptitude. Some will be men of science, others of art, others still, of action. But over all the inclinations which may bind you severally to different tasks and ways of life, you should guard in your inner soul the consciousness of the fundamental unity of our nature, which demands that every human being be, above and before all, the unspoiled pattern of a man in whom no noble faculty of the mind be obliterated, and no lofty interest for all men have lost its communicative virtue. Before all modifications of profession and training stands the fulfilment of the destiny common to all rational beings. "There is one universal profession:—to be a man," says Guyau.[4]

Rodó urges youth to develop "not a single aspect, but the plenitude of its being: to be spectators where they may not be actors." "Our capacity to understand," he says, "must be limited only by the impossibility of understanding souls that are narrow." Rodó is aware that in the dichotomy of civilization—a high level of culture and a high degree of specialization—lies the greatest threat to a society. The specialized eye has a narrow and distorted vision of the world: ". . . it injures the spirit of human solidarity by the particularization of individual habits and affections."[5]

In this context Rodó quotes Auguste Comte, who spoke of "brains very efficient under one aspect and monstrously inept under all others," thus coming uncannily close to describing the tragic spectacle of the atomic scientist, both feared and admired by his contemporaries and insulated by his own society. For contrast we need only focus our attention anew on Greek culture. According to Macaulay, ". . . a day in the public life of Athens comprised a more brilliant programme of instruction than any we now plan in our modern centres of education."[6]

We must spare time, then, for ideal contemplation and disinterested thinking; we must protect our souls from mutilation by the tyranny of a single and self-interested goal; we must never justify enslaving the soul by means of absorption in work or in conflict; our human integrity must be maintained. No one function should ever prevail over the final achievement. The duty and pleasure of man is to think, to dream, and to admire: this is what the ancients called *otium*, the use of time for purposes other than mere economic activity and the very core of a higher life.

The practical modern man, the "utilitarian," will invariably attempt to destroy the sense of beauty in others. We must make art the basic element in our culture; the appreciation of beauty is a promise that we will arrive at the understanding of justice: "Never does a man more surely fulfil his duty than when he feels it, not as an imposition, but as part of a beautiful harmony."[7]

The identification of the just with the beautiful is typical of Renan, Taine, and Guyau. Rodó has a deep faith in the concept: "In the measure that humanity progresses it sees that the moral law is but beauty of conduct; it shows evil and error like a discord; and will seek for the good as a restored harmony."[8]

Rodó believed that the ideal civilization was a combination of Christian charity and the classic cult of beauty: "The perfection of human morality would be to cast the spirit of charity in the moulds of Grecian elegance."[9] This idea, however, is not acceptable to the utilitarian, to whom every act must bring an immediate profit. This attitude is produced by the revelations of natural science and the universal acceptance of the democratic ideal. Led by his distrust of democracy, which he considered a leveling force working toward mediocrity, Rodó follows the ideology of Renan, who maintains that "high preoccupation with the ideal interests of our race is irreconcilable with the spirit of democracy." Other French thinkers of the last century agree with him. Bourget, for instance, thinks that the "universal triumph of democratic institutions will make civilization lose in profundity what it gains in extension." Rodó carries these ideas to a more obvious conclusion:

Abandoned to itself, without the constant rectification of some active moral sanction which shall purify and guide its motives to the dignifying of life—democracy will, gradually, extinguish the idea of any superiority which may not be turned into a more efficient training of the war of interests. It is then the most ignoble form of the brutalities of power. Spiritual preference, exaltation of life by unselfish motive, good taste and art and manners, and the admiration of all that is worthy and of good repute, will then alike vanish unprotected when social equality has destroyed all grades of excellence without replacing them with others that shall also rule by moral influence and the light of reason.[10]

Democracy, however, is not this negative force, since the "affirmation of democracy and its glory consist in arousing in itself by fit incentives the revelation and the mastery of the true superiority of men."[11] We must, therefore, uphold the concept of human superiorities and legitimate merits. The advocates of mediocrity will hate merit and label it rebellion: ". . . they will call the dogmatism of common sense, wisdom; mean avidness of heart, gravity; adaptation to the mediocre, sound judgment; and bad taste, manly indifference to trifles."[12]

Próspero, that is, Rodó, warns his disciples against these Philistines:

And if you make a prophet of your neighbour who preaches the belittling lesson of the mediocre, if you make him your hero and seek your salvation in his bureaucratic content, you will encounter that rancorous, implacable hostility against all that is beautiful, all that is dignified or delicate in the spirit of humanity which, even more than its brutal shedding of blood, is so repugnant in the Jacobite tyranny. Before its tribunal the wisdom of a Lavoisier, the genius of a Chenier, the dignity of a Malesherbes, become only faults; amid the shouting of its Conventions we hear the cry, Distrust that man, he has written a book![13]

Fear of the egalitarian tyranny and predominance of the masses is evident in all the great thinkers of the century. Comte saw in democratic equality only a transitory elimination of ancient class systems; Renan accepted only the Athenian concept of equality, "an equality of demigods"; Taine denounced the invasion of the heights by the multitude; Carlyle wrote against irreverent leveling and in favor of heroism; and Emerson echoed this idea in the bosom of "the most positivist of democracies." Flaubert decries mediocrity animated by the spirit of leveling and the tyranny of the masses. Ibsen—in the words of Stockmann—declares that compact majorities are the greatest threat to liberty and truth; and, against the ideal of a "mediatized" humanity, Nietzsche pits the concept of a superman who surges above the common level with the thrust of a tidal wave.

Despite these opinions, Rodó affirms that the spirit of democracy is essential to our civilization and that it would be idle to revolt against it. Democracy does have elements that are "final" and "fruitful," and even if it has not yet reconciled the principle of equality with the principle of selectivity, we should not fail to recognize its real worth.

Rodó and the idealistic thinkers of his time worried about the ultimate fate of the spirit of selectiveness. They were aware that democracy exalts mediocrity and rejects intellectual superiority—that is, refinement, sensibility, and acceptance of the higher forms of culture. The task ahead is to persuade the masses that there are different cultural levels, to educate them further and thus bring about the acknowledgment of these natural categories. Popular education, based on a sense of order and a will to achieve justice, is the means to imparting this knowledge.

We must avoid confusing equality of opportunity

and actual equality among the members of a society:

> The true and worthy notion of equality rests on the assumption that all reasonable beings are endowed by nature with faculties capable of a noble development. The duty of the State consists in seeing that all its members are so placed as to be able to seek without favour their own "best"; in so arranging things as to bring to light each human superiority, wherever it exists.[14]

The spirit of emulation, the product of intellectual energy and free will, is sure to produce a greatness of the mind not inherited but natural; "the most powerful spur of all that urge to action, as well in thought as in other human activities, needs as well equality at the starting-point in order to produce at the finish that inequality which gives the palm to the apter scholar or the greater man."[15]

There is no room for the abuses of aristocracy once the equality of man is unchallenged in all realms except those of intelligence and virtue. As Fouillée would say, "The great law of natural selection will go on functioning in human society only so long as it works more and more on a basis of liberty."

However, warns Rodó, we do not oppose a Nietzschean notion to the egalitarianism that would bring every man to a common level. From a genuinely Christian point of view, Rodó states that moral superiority implies duties: "Each superior being owes to others more in proportion to his excess in ability over them."[16]

As early as 1899 Rodó realized that Nietzsche's an-

tidemocratic views led his "abominable and reaction-
ary genius" to the vindication of what he calls natural
rights, implicit in human superiorities:

. . . for, in scoffing at all mercy, all fraternity, he places in the
heart of the superman he deifies a Satanic disregard of the
weak and the disinherited; he legitimizes all privileges of
self-will and force to governments of the gibbet and the lash,
and with resolution comes to his keynote: "Society does not
exist for itself, but for its elect."[17]

Rodó anticipated the infamous Nazi conception of society that was to be based on the spurious notion of
racial superiority and built on the lethal scheme of
thought control and concentration camps. For Rodó,
"love" is the only possible basis of any social order.
Only those who possess the true capacity to love
should rule.

Equality of opportunity and selection of the best
qualified, of those endowed with the virtues of mind
and character, are the pillars of Rodó's democracy.
The "new" science seems to bear him out, for it reveals how "the principle of democracy may be reconciled with an aristocracy of morals or of culture in the
organization of human collectivities."[18]

In agreement with Henri Béranger, Rodó maintains that the affirmations of science contribute to
sanctioning and fortifying the idea of democracy and,
like Christianity, exalt the dignity of the apparently
minor contributor. This new thought, accepted by
Rodó, ascribes the building of the foundations of ge-
ology to the labor of the infinitely small nummulite

and bryozoan at the bottom of the sea; it derives from the vibration of a formless primitive cell all the elevating impulses of organized life; it shows the great role played in our psychology by vague and inconspicuous phenomena, even the fugitive perceptions of our subconscious self; in sociology and history, it restores to the masses their share of heroism that was ignored in glorifying the individual hero; and it reveals the slow accumulation of personal research that, in obscure workshops or laboratories of forgotten toilers, has prepared the discoveries of genius.

Conversely, however, science shows that progress requires leadership amid the immense mass of persons and things. From the postulates of science and the observation of order in nature will evolve the new society that will harmonize two historical forces destined to give our civilization its true character: the sentiment of equality created by Christianity, and the sense of order and authority—the respect for genius—that comes from our Greek heritage. The future will see the synthesis of these two basic principles; then and only then will democracy achieve its final triumph.

After considering democracy in general, Rodó examines the United States.

The utilitarian conception as the idea of human destiny, and equality *at* the mediocre as the norm of social proportion, make up the formula which in Europe they call the spirit of Americanism. If one could say of utilitarianism that it is the word of the English spirit, the United States may be considered the incarnation of that word.[19]

The Latin-American power elites and even the masses greatly admire the success of the United States: "The mighty confederation is realizing over us a sort of moral conquest," says Rodó.

As a preliminary to his critical analysis of the North American cultural body, Rodó salutes the great nation. He praises its traditional liberty and its spirit of unity and organization. He commends it for having revealed the total greatness and dignity of labor, for its insatiable curiosity, and for its unbending faith in public education. He admires a culture identified with the practical, one forever applying science to new inventions, a society with an uncanny gift for improvisation. He is impressed with the religious spirit of the nation and with a certain primitive robustness even amidst the refinements of a highly civilized life:

They hold to the pagan cult of health, sanity, and strength; they preserve in strong muscles the instrument of a strong will; obliged by their insatiable ambition to employ all human energies, they fit the torso of the athlete over the heart of the free man. And from all this springs a dominant note of optimism, confidence, faith, which makes them face the future with a proud and stubborn assurance; the note of "Excelsior" and the "Psalm of Life," which their poets have opposed as a balsam to melancholy or bitterness of spirit.[20]

About these virtues Rodó candidly states: "I do not love them, but I admire them. I admire them, first, for their formidable power of *desire*; I bow before that school of will and work." Rodó finds this element of will, of the supreme energy, even in figures considered exceptional within the culture, such as Poe, who rebelled against his society and vainly struggled to express himself from an infinite solitude. The "fundamental note . . . in the character of Poe's heroes is still the inner shrine, the unconquerable resistance of the will. When he imagined Ligeia, most mysterious and adorable of his creatures, he symbolized in the inextinguishable light of her eyes the hymn of man's will over death."[21] Had Rodó been acquainted with Melville's writings he would have found in *Moby Dick* the perfect example of that indomitable will; for the will that took Ahab to meet his death is the perfect symbol of this American trait.

Having praised the positive aspects of the American nation, Rodó discusses the less flattering aspects. The first question that comes to his mind is this: "Does the American society realize, or at least tend to realize, the ideal of such rational conduct as satisfies, to the heart's desire, the intellectual and moral dignity of our civilization?"[22] His answer is negative: "Its prosperity is as immense as its incapability of satisfying even a mediocre view of human destiny."[23]

Material wealth allows the American to assuage his vanity by acquiring material luxury, but this occurs outside the farthest confines of good taste. Art can hardly exist in such a society except as the rebellion of an individual, and Poe and Emerson are strangers to the American environment. An American may spend fortunes in artistic treasures, "but he has never felt the divine frenzy of poem or picture."[24] "The ideal of beauty does not appeal to the descendants of the austere Puritan."[25]

In educational matters, "their [the Americans'] . . . praiseworthy efforts to extend the benefits of popular education are inspired with the noble motive of communicating the rudiments of knowledge to the masses; but it does not appear that they also concern themselves overmuch with that higher education which shall rise above the general mediocrity."[26]

Rodó detects a retrogression of intellectual activity from the times of the Declaration of Independence and the Constitution, from the days of Emerson, Channing, and Poe up to the time of his book. At the turn of the century magazines and periodicals had replaced good books or the immortal *Federalist*.

Rodó was writing in 1900. Sixty-one years later, *Time, Life,* and *Look* constitute preferential reading in the United States. These mammoth-circulation magazines are the current providers of intellectual substance for the great American public. Of course, the selection is incomplete and unfair, as was Rodó's.

Rodó's views on religion in the United States would probably be rejected by most Americans; for instance, he tells us that "American religiosity is merely an auxiliary force for the penal law."[27] In other words, it is the utilitarian morality, the essence of which is found in Benjamin Franklin:

. . . a philosophy of conduct which has for its goal a commonplace sagacity, a prudent usefulness, in whose bosom will never rise the emotions of holiness or heroism; and which, fit only to give to one's conscience in the common affairs of life a certain moral support—like the apple-tree cane with which Franklin ever walked—is but a fragile staff with which to surmount great heights.[28]

Rodó next proceeds to examine the political power of a plutocracy composed of the constituents and agents of trusts and monopolies, the lords and minions of economic life. The principle of the struggle for life reigns supreme, and its worshipers become the embodiment of national energy.

When Rodó was writing *Ariel,* the West had just become the great magnet for the American people: ". . . the West, where the most faithful representation of American life is to be found at this moment of its evolution."[29] All the shortcomings of a pseudodemocracy will become more flagrant there. Chicago will rule, and the old traditions of the Mayflower colonists, the patricians of Virginia, the New England gentlemen, and the lawmakers of the Emancipation will live only in the older states.

With the increase of material wealth will come a desire to spread the American gospel all over the world. "Today," writes Rodó in 1900, "they openly aspire to the primacy of the world's civilization, the direction of its ideas, and think themselves the forerunners of all culture that is to prevail."[30]

Americans base their right to cultural rivalry with Europe on a feeling of superiority that will soon leave their achievements behind. They will not believe that in spite of their inventions and material advance, they do not of themselves suffice to alter the axis of the earth.

The question is not one of cultural deficiency only:

. . . their own character precludes all possibility of their supremacy. Nature has not granted them the genius for propaganda, the vocation of the apostle. They lack the great gift of *amiability,* likableness, in a lofty sense; that extraordinary power of sympathy with which those races endowed by Providence for the task of education know how to make of their culture a beauty, as did Greece, lovable, eternal and yet always with something of their own.[31]

After making such assertions Rodó seems repentant and willing to give utilitarianism its due: "All history shows a definite relation of growth between the progress of utilitarian activity and the ideal."[32] The work of North American positivism will thus eventually serve the cause of Ariel.

Rodó concludes his considerations on North American culture with a note of vague optimism:

The relation between material good and good that is intellectual or moral is thus only a new aspect of that modern doctrine which we call the transformation of energy; material well-being may be transformed into spiritual superiority. But North American life does not as yet offer us any example of this indisputable relation, nor even dimly suggest it as the triumph of the generation to come.[33]

Let us hope, then, that the spirit of that Titanic organism, which so far has been utility and will-power only, may some day also be intelligence, sentiment, ideality; that from that mighty forge may arise, in last result, the noble human figure, harmonious, select. . . .[34]

Having serenely expressed his hopes of a better future, Rodó leaves the United States, not without warning Latin America against the dangers of imitating its spirit of materialism and easy success. He then turns his eyes anew toward his own countries and allows them to linger on the vast panorama of the cities. New idealistic thoughts rush to his mind, and he writes: "In this view that city only is great whose spirit's barriers extend far beyond the mountains or the seas, whose very name pronounced illuminates for posterity an epoch of human thought, a horizon of history."[35] Rodó considers the great cities of Latin America and asks himself if they also have a hollow sound and will finally end like Tyre or Sidon, or as Carthage ended. He hopes that such a fate will not be theirs, that the younger generations will prevent a similar end. Our salvation is in the future: "The past belonged entirely to the sword arm; the present seems well-nigh given over to the horny hand that clears away and builds; the future shall offer the stability, the scenario, the right atmosphere, to make possible the higher evolution of man's soul."[36]

The new Latin America, noble and generous, is in sight. Rodó tells his students that perhaps they will be only the forerunners of the new America. Rodó has now become the apostle of the future: "The future is, in the life of human societies, the one inspiring thought."[37]

The school of pessimism headed by Hartmann believes in "going on with the work of improvement, labouring for the good of the future, so that human effort, aiding evolution, may bring about a more rapid impulse to the final end—which is the termination of all sorrow, and likewise of all life."[38] Contrary to Hartmann, Rodó talks to his disciples on behalf of hope and life and asks them to labor for the future. Because he is pleading such an excellent cause, the Master has sought inspiration in the image of Ariel: "Ariel is reason and the higher truth. Ariel is that sublime sentiment of the perfectibility of man." Ariel stands for idealism and order in life, lofty inspiration in thought, generosity in conduct, good taste in art, courage in action, and delicacy and refinement in manners and usages.[39]

Próspero ends his talk to his students with an explanation of the word *Esperanza* and a call to the eternal cult of the ideal symbolized by Ariel.

Rodó's ideas about modern society are often mistakenly labeled "antidemocratic." Havelock Ellis, Rodó's kindred spirit, provides a more accurate interpretation of these ideas:

It will be seen that, alike in his criticism of life and his criteria of progress, Rodó remains essentially democratic. He is altogether out of sympathy with the antidemocratic conception of life often associated with Nietzsche's doctrine of the super-man. He waved politely aside the affirmation of Bourget that the triumph of democracy would mean the defeat of civilization, and greatly as he admired the genius of Renan, he refused to believe that a concern for ideal interests is opposed to the democratic spirit; such a belief, indeed, would be the condemnation of Latin America as much as of

Anglo-Saxon America. Rodó accepts democracy, but on that basis, he insists on the need for selection. Even in Nature, he remarks, among flowers and insects and birds and onwards, we see natural selection favouring superiority and ensuring the triumph of beauty. It is not the destruction but the education of democracy which is needed in order to further this process of natural selection. Rodó held that it is the duty of the State to render possible the uniform revelation of human superiorities wherever they exist. Democracy alone can conciliate equality at the outset with an inequality at the end which gives full scope for the best and most apt to work towards the good of the whole.[40]

Rodó was of the tribe of Quinet and Renan, of Fouillée and especially Guyau. Like those fine spirits, he desired to be the messenger of sweetness and of light, of the spirit of Jesus combined with the spirit of Athens, and the intolerance of rationalism seemed to him as deadly a poison to civilization as that of Christianity. In his steady devotion to this combined ideal Rodó may be said to be European, and more distinctly French. But in his adaptation of that ideal to the needs of his own land, and his firm establishment of it on a democratic basis, he is the representative of South America. It was his final hope that out of the agony of this war (the war of 1914) there would emerge new ideals of life, new aspirations of art, in which Latin America, stirred by the worldwide shock, would definitely affirm its own conscious personality.[41]

Sixty years after the publication of *Ariel,* we may ask ourselves how right Rodó was in his judgment of North American culture. I would say candidly that he was right, that America, with all its wealth, progress, and vitality, is still groping in the darkness of a formless idealism, still holding to a tradition of utilitarianism, still more interested in the present than in the future. In the twentieth century North America has had the possibility of becoming the leader of the world; at this very moment what we call the free world looks to the United States for salvation. This nation, however, has not been able to conquer its limitations, to shape its noble impulses, to dissociate ideal motives from material interests. Wealth and military strength, even good intentions, are not enough to counteract the inroads of new ideologies, of new forces in motion all over the world.

Was Rodó's judgment of Latin America correct? I would say frankly, no. Latin America has not fulfilled the hopes created by Rodó's vision of that continent. Democracy has failed in most of the Latin-American countries. It would be a mockery to speak of aesthetic ideals, of *otium,* among illiterate and oppressed peoples; even Christian charity is an exotic plant in Latin America, hence the utter misery of half of its population. Political demagogues have adopted most of Rodó's ideas to use them at election time or in the hollow chambers of congress; and yet, the message of the Uruguayan thinker is very much alive, and we must believe in it, despite bitter realities. I believe with Rodó that North America will transform its materialistic impulses into purer forms of existence, even though that transformation may be accomplished in the distant future, and that out of its own ruined societies, Latin America will build the noble architecture of the new world.

Some Notes on the Literary Influence of the United States in Spanish-American Letters

ANY attempt to discuss North American influences on the literature of Hispanic America is a thorny and highly debatable matter. Western literature is such an intricate crisscross of influences that any elementary appraisal of them can easily lead to naïve oversimplification. If we mistake simple resemblance for influence, it would take volumes to cover the distance between Franklin and Saroyan, but if we hold to the true concept of influence, we could say that only Edgar Allan Poe and, in a lesser degree, Walt Whitman, have really left a mark on the body of our literature.

When I speak of influences in literary matters I have in mind the "action" of one writer on another, or of one school or tendency on another school or tendency. Such a phenomenon implies intellectual ascendancy.

When a literary body borrows characteristics from an alien literature it is bound to lose some of its own traditional traits. It can no longer follow an independent course. Such a loss occurred to Spanish romanticism, specifically in the cases of Martínez de la Rosa, Espronceda, and even Larra. The same situation is true of Spanish-American romanticism. I offer no moral or utilitarian considerations on the subject. These are merely facts.

Such pervasive influences as romanticism, the *parnasse,* symbolism, naturalism, and surrealism have come into our literature from France. In some instances a single French author has conditioned the work of many Spanish Americans. Such was the case with Victor Hugo, Leconte de Lisle, Balzac, Baudelaire, Verlaine, Zola, Laforgue, Samain, and Apollinaire. Rubén Darío "awoke" to poetry under the spell of Victor Hugo; contact with the French poet brought about the first change in his poetic manner. Leconte de Lisle conditioned the aesthetic approach of Leopoldo Díaz; Balzac was the undisputed master of Blest Gana; Baudelaire altered the creative course of Julián del Casal; Verlaine intimately affected the poetic expression of Amado Nervo and Darío; Zola is without a doubt the literary progenitor of Federico Gamboa; Laforgue and Samain had a profound effect on the work of Herrera y Reissig; and Apollinaire is surely the mentor of Vicente Huidobro.

To what extent has North American literature reacted upon the sensibility of our writers? What new vibrations has it produced among them? Has it created a new aesthetic climate for them? Has contact with the North produced new forms of expression? These are some of the pertinent questions. I think that it is rather difficult to answer them with any degree of accuracy. I would say even that it is impossible to establish the true depth of North American literary penetration in South America. The problem in the field of poetry, moreover, is not at all the same as that in the field of prose—be it the novel, essay, or play.

The essentials of lyric poetry are to be sought in individual sensitivity, cultural tradition, racial sentiment, feeling for language, and command of style. Consequently, external influences are bound to come from kindred literatures—Mediterranean or Latin literatures, in our particular circumstances. North American perception is expressed in a manner far removed from ours; the cultural traditions of the United States are foreign to us; its ideals are often diametrically opposed to ours; the sounds of its language tend to bewilder rather than please us. It is no wonder, then, that it is difficult to know, appreciate, and accept a poet from North America.

Our academic writers did flirt with one of them, however. His lyric inanities and cool clichés were rendered into Spanish, but, except for some junior high school teachers, nobody remembers Longfellow these days. There are no traces of his platitudes in our poetry. There is another poet whose superb artistry penetrated much deeper and to this day continues to be studied: Edgar Allan Poe. Poe's masterful analysis of the creative process remains a lasting contribution to our literary techniques.[1] His eerie tales and frantic geometric poems left a distinguished progeny. No one would deny his influence on Leopoldo Díaz, Darío, Silva, Lugones, Herrera y Reissig, and Quiroga. All in all, however, his influence was sporadic and limited in scope. There is little, if anything, for example, from the poet of "The Raven," in Gutiérrez Nájera, Nervo, or González Martínez.[2] Poe did not succeed in creating a lasting lyric climate or even a lasting poetic formula.

Still another poet was not only acclaimed and translated but also plagiarized. Whitman was a sort of literary hurricane who swept the South—wrecking, creating, distorting, fertilizing, and vitiating. His enumerative style led to a grinding word motorization such as we find in Ronald de Carvalho or in the Lugones of *Las montañas del oro.* Darío did admire Whitman—witness his "Soneto a Whitman"—nevertheless he could hardly have been swayed by the northern poet, whose work was the opposite of his fine ornamental verse. Darío belongs to the tradition of the *parnasse;* he could easily be the archetype of the Latin poet. Whitman is the Yankee poet. Although at times grandiose, as in his elegy to Lincoln, "When Lilacs Last in the Dooryard Bloom'd," he is often prosaic, wordy, and given to lengthy enumeration. Darío is poetic even when at his most robust and virile—for example, in "A Roosevelt" and "Salutación del optimista." This fact is evident in every element of his work—form, word, rhythm, image. Both Whitman and Darío are bold and striking, but whereas the Yankee is deeply human, the Nicaraguan is not only that but divine as well. It is easy to understand Darío's admiration of Whitman; influence is out of the question.

On the other hand, Whitman's power over Lugones, a veritable poetic weather vane, is not hard to explain. Lugones followed Hugo, Leconte de Lisle, Laforgue, Baudelaire, Poe, Darío, and Lautréamont; but the North American's influence was not deep or lasting, and the exquisite author of *El libro de los paisajes* or the virile poet of *El romancero* shows nothing of Whitman. There are no traces, either, of the author of *Leaves of Grass* in José Santos Chocano, except for a certain petulance: "Let Whitman have the North, I have the South," the Peruvian bard once said. In Díaz Mirón there is no indication of influence unless it be unleashed arrogance. One would be hard put to it, moreover, to detect any Whitman in Julián del Casal, Gutiérrez Nájera, or any of the *modernistas*.

Walt Whitman's influence is a twentieth-century phenomenon. It can be said that Sabat Ercasty, Pablo Neruda, León Felipe, Ronald de Carvalho, and other excellent poets were his disciples at one time or another. They seem to share his "cosmic conscience," his taste for grandeur in rhetoric, and his penchant for chaotic word lists. These dangerous traits are found even in those who translate him, not to mention minor poets aching to grow, or simply practicers of the genre who tend to think that poetry and grandiloquence are one and the same thing. The Alexander translation of Whitman's complete poetic works may well turn the tide and channel the current of Whitman's influence, thus clearing light formal debris from the literary stream. Only then will the great poet's ideals, his feeling for humanity, and his vital joy shine through the writings of those who submit to him.

Literary influences are at best a slippery subject. Often the critic is carried away by his own theories and exaggerates more or less alarmingly, if not out of all proportion. Mariano Latorre evidently was so impelled when he wrote an essay entitled "Bret Harte y el criollismo sudamericano":

The nationalistic feeling in American literature springs from significant personalities fired by unexpected events, i.e., revolution or economic immigration, and it began concretely with Bret Harte's *Bocetos californianos*. The Pacific coast followed the trend long after Bret Harte. The new feeling, for such it was, came to them through his literary heirs, men like Jack London and Curwood, through writers from Uruguay, Chile and Argentina, and, finally, through the Messianic and social urges of the Russian novelists—Gorki in particular.[3]

In Latorre's opinion, any story dealing with miners, adventurers, Gauchos, farm hands, or *rotos,* any inkling of sensitivity to social phenomena in the narrative, or any use of the vernacular stems from Bret Harte's example; thus, he has made strange bedfellows of Acevedo Díaz, Lynch, Guiraldes, Federico Gana, Manuel Rojas, and some twenty writers just as basically dissimilar. It might be wiser to look for traces of Zola, Maupassant, or Sarmiento among these writers.

For taking one's bearings on the choppy seas of literary influences two methods seem advisable. One would lead us first to survey the outstanding contemporary writers, including Alfonso Reyes, Gabriela Mistral, Rómulo Gallegos, González Martínez, Pedro Henríquez Ureña, Ricardo Rojas, Pablo Neruda, Borges, Eduardo Mallea, Pedro Prado, Eduardo Barrios, Juana de Ibarbourou, and Manuel Bandeira. The next step would be to track down whatever North American literary influences are to be found in these writers. This task might be a fruitless one. It would be possible to detect admiration for Whitman and Sherwood Anderson in Mallea's work, or perhaps even to sense his yearning to be under their particular magic, but nothing beyond wishful thinking could be proven. Pedro Henríquez Ureña was a true connoisseur of American literature, but his interest was strictly scholarly. Pablo Neruda tends to avail himself of some of Whitman's resources, to cultivate free verse, and to indulge in enumerative techniques. The rest of these authors have not been appreciably touched by North American literature.

The other method would start with the alleged source of influence; we could begin with outstanding writers of the United States: Caldwell, Dos Passos, Dreiser, Farrell, Faulkner, Hemingway, Lewis, O'Neill, Steinbeck, Eliot, Pound, Frost, Katherine Anne Porter, and others. What characteristics of their work do we find in the Spanish-American writers? If we find any it would be desirable to look into the work of the latter. Is it really good or is it simply mediocre? Are these literary figures merely disseminators of artistic formulas, easy targets for stylistic novelties or thematic innovations? If so, we need not worry: there is no problem.

Utterly misleading in this pursuit are the presence of aesthetic mannerisms, special subject matter, and peculiar types and attitudes that have invaded the western literatures at given moments. It could be that any resemblance between James Fenimore Cooper and our writers of historical novels is merely coincidental and that further literary sleuthing would take us beyond the man who wrote *The Last of the Mohicans* and lead us to none other than Sir Walter Scott.

It is a well-established fact that Poe became known in Spanish America through Mallarmé and Baudelaire. There must be something French, some impalpable Gallic element, in their renditions of that poet's work. Mariano Latorre read Bret Harte in French, and it is not unlikely that the translations slanted to some extent the style of the California storyteller. What is true of Poe and Bret Harte is also true of Whitman; many a Spanish-American writer has become acquainted with him through French versions. It is possible that the same may be true today of Faulkner, Eliot, Pound, or O'Neill. Of far greater importance, however, is the question of how we may spot the influence of Proust, Dostoevski, Kafka, Mallarmé, George, Joyce, Virginia Woolf, Laforgue, Gide, Romains, Apollinaire, Paul

Valéry, Reverdy, or Breton in the writer from the United States.

When confronted with a case of apparent influence in a specific work, the shrewd critic will have to answer these questions. Does one detect traces of Cooper, Chateaubriand, or Sir Walter Scott? Does the work give the impression of the influence of Poe or Baudelaire—or of Faulkner or Kafka?

At this point it might be wise to remember that the writer in question must have some original talent produced and cultivated in his own habitat. It is quite legitimate to state that Jorge Isaacs is reminiscent of Chateaubriand, but it is also fair to add that there were reasons for resemblance: both men had similar temperaments, similar education, somewhat similar family life, and both lived in close contact with nature. It is quite possible that Baldomero Lillo did not have Bret Harte in mind when he wrote about the miners among whom he lived. Is it a writer's doing if the sea life in Patagonia resembles the sea life in Jack London's Klondike? We can hardly draw momentous conclusions from the faint similarity between the Gauchos in the novels of Acevedo Díaz or Javier de Viana and O. Henry's Texans. It is possible for Darío to be under the spell of the mysterious without owing his fascination to Edgar Allan Poe's raven. It is quite within the realm of probability for the writers of Ecuador or Mexico to apprehend and convey the social realities of their countries without reference to Upton Sinclair or John Steinbeck. Mallea's introspection is his own. Neruda's nerves and glands may be as much responsible for his literary proclivities as this or that influence. Those nerves and glands are the true reason for the grandiose rhetorical sweep in his reaction to the spectacle of life.

It would appear that in order to reach a reasonably valid conclusion, the critic should avoid any type of ironclad thesis, tempting as it may be. Perhaps the most sensible starting point is the realization that literature is an expression of the life around us, that most of the "great" differences among men are circumstantial, and that the world is evolving toward unity and community in the realms of thought and interests, sad as this reflection may be.

In 1920, Pedro Henríquez Ureña wrote an excellent review of J. de L. Ferguson's *American Literature in Spain.*[4] "Ferguson assumes that the literature of the United States has been widely popular and very influential in Spanish America," he writes in the opening paragraph. "It is certain that investigation would yield the very opposite conclusion."[5] This point of view is a very valid one, and we shall return to it.

No neophyte in the field, Henríquez Ureña brought a good deal of light to bear on the question of literary influence. He looks keenly into the work of Enrique Díez Canedo, who translated the most outstanding poets of the generation of 1914: Stephen Crane, Ezra Pound,

Edgar Lee Masters, Carl Sandburg, and Gould Fletcher. He examines the labors of translators and critics in Spanish America: the Spanish version of Longfellow's poems done by Blanco Fombona and by Merchán, a Cuban who undertook the translation of *Evangeline;* Amado Nervo's translation of Whitman's work; and the studies made by Salomón de la Selva in an effort to introduce such poets as William Rose Benét, Edna St. Vincent Millay, Markham, Masters, Sandburg, Lindsay, Frost, and Amy Lowell to the Spanish-speaking reader.

Henríquez Ureña goes on to mention José Martí's essays on Emerson and Whitman (which have the distinction of being the first in Spanish); and Varona's essays on Emerson (1884), on Poe and Baudelaire—the piece on the two poets was part of *Desde mi Belvedere* (1907)—and on Emerson and Renan (1903), later incorporated into *Violetas y ortigas* (1917). Other works briefly examined by Henríquez Ureña are *Los grandes poetas norteamericanos,*[6] by Balbió Dávalos; Rubén Darío's article on Edgar Allan Poe;[7] *Poetas muertos en la guerra,* an anthology by Pedro Requena Legarreta;[8] and the translations of Mark Twain's short stories, *Cuentos,* by J. Fernández McGregor.[9] Lastly he comments on *Las Novedades* and *Inter America,* two New York magazines to which we owe much in matters of literary exchange. Of all the writers here examined there is only one in whose poetry we find American stylistic traces: Salomón de la Selva.

Pedro Henríquez Ureña was exceedingly well informed on North American literature. As early as 1909 he was writing an article on playwright Clyde Fitch, later incorporated into his book, *Horas de estudio*. While in this country he wrote on Edith Wharton, William Rose Benét, Vachel Lindsay, and Edna St. Vincent Millay.

His article "Veinte años de literatura en los Estados Unidos" is perhaps the best short survey of American literature published in the first quarter of this century.[10] A paragraph from his foreword will give us an idea about this remarkable essay:

In the course of this rapid survey of North American literature I will look into groups, movements and orientations. To enumerate and evaluate authors individually would be tiresome for readers not necessarily well acquainted with them. Those whose work I will take up will also illustrate significant moments in the literary life of the United States.[11]

His choices provide intelligent guidance and often reveal unbelievable intuition, as well as broad knowledge. His findings in the field are to be found in his book *Literary Currents in Spanish America*.[12]

The Ecuadoran Francisco Alexander completed the first entire translation of *Leaves of Grass* in 1955. Mr. Alexander maintains that it is wrong to attempt a partial translation of the work. Despite its many facets, it is, in his estimation, a single poem. Whether or not one agrees with him, the extraordinary quality of his effort is evident. He rendered also Whitman's introductions to the many editions of *Leaves of Grass* (1872, 1885, 1891). Thanks to Alexander, we have a vital set of documents that reveals the literary theories of the American poet and presents his understanding of human motivation, his love of freedom and democracy, and his religious principles.

Alexander's translation captures the beauty underlying Whitman's poetry. Its rhythm, verbal richness, and symbolism are as alive as the feeling that permeates the whole of the original. This has been accomplished without straying from the text. Mr. Alexander has attained this success in spite of Whitman's elemental enumeration of verbs, adjectives, and nouns; his changeable syntax; and his predilection for the gerund. This book will add greatly to the popularity of the North American poet in the Hispanic and Hispanic-American world.

Leaves of Grass appeared in 1855. Since then its reputation has been increasing steadily in Spanish America. Since 1887, when José Martí revealed the poet's work to a wide public, hundreds of pieces on Walt Whitman have been written. The greater part of the bibliography, nevertheless, belongs to our century. Armando Vasseur was the first of Whitman's translators. He was followed by Arturo Torres-Ríoseco (1922-46), León Felipe (1941), and José Gabriel y Francisco Alexander (1955).

Alexander's book is the best. The least authentic and most poetic version is León Felipe's.[13]

Fernando Alegría has written a study on Whitman,[14] discussing the following aspects of the poet's work: biography, *Leaves of Grass,* the basic ideas of Walt Whitman, the sexual problem, Whitman's influence on

Spanish-American poetry, and Whitman in translation. This book is sure to be influential among the young intellectuals in South America.

John Englekirk has written the most significant work about Poe.[15] In it he discusses the better-known translations of Poe's poems. Of these translations I favor the 1887 version of "The Raven" by Pérez Bonalde and various translations of Poe's works done by the Argentine poets, Leopoldo Díaz and Carlos Obligado. Enrique Piñeyro (1877) was one of the first literary critics in Spanish America to study Poe. He was followed by Santiago Pérez Triana (1887), Rubén Darío (1893), Enrique José Varona (1895), Balbino Dávalos (1901), and others.

Dr. Englekirk analyzes Poe's influence on Leopoldo Díaz, Rubén Darío, Silva, del Casal, Gutiérrez Nájera, Amado Nervo, Lugones, Jaimes Freyre, Herrera y Reissig, Horacio Quiroga, Arévalo Martínez, Chocano, Eguren, de Greiff, and a few other and less important poets. This book represents the most serious effort to date to study the fate of the great American poet in the Spanish-speaking world. Dr. Englekirk has assembled an impressive amount of bibliography, undoubtedly very much alive these days, since interest in the poetry of Edgar Allan Poe is still increasing.

In his short essay dealing with "magical realism" in the Spanish-American novel, Ángel Flores has discussed

Poe's contribution to this particular literary approach:

Obviously the most persistent influence then was Edgar Allan Poe, either directly or via his admirers, especially the French decadents grouped as *Los raros* by Darío: Baudelaire, Barbey d'Aurevilly, Villiers de l'Isle Adam, etc. This imaginative writing found its way into the twentieth century and is discernible in the prose experiments of many gifted poets: in México, Jaime Torres Bodet's *Margarita de Niebla* (1927) and *Proserpina rescatada* (1931), in Xavier Villaurrutia's *Dama de corazones* (1928), in Gilberto Owen's *Novela en forma de nube* (1928), and in Salvador Novo's *Return Ticket* (1928); in Peru, in Abraham Valdelomar's novels and in *El caballero Carmelo y otros cuentos* (1918), and in Martín Adán's *La casa de cartón* (1929); in Argentina, most especially in those nightmares of anarchy and tumult entitled *El juguete rabioso* (1926), *Los siete locos* (1929), and *Los Lanzallamas* (1931) by Roberto Arlt.[16]

Mallea is thoroughly familiar with English and North American literature. There are strains of Walt Whitman in his *La Bahía de Silencio;* there is a translation of a Whitman poem in his *Historia de una pasión argentina;* and there are references to Camden in his *Nocturno europeo* and in his *La ciudad junto al río inmóvil.* Waldo Frank is a close friend of Mallea and there are ideological similarities between the two. Frank is the proponent of a cultural synthesis of New York and Buenos Aires and believes in the necessity of having an "order" in society. The medieval stratification, based on function, is his ideal. Mallea shares his enthusiasm, and when he speaks of "legitimate categories" he means an order based on the natural articulation of the individual. Like Frank, he is in favor of a "new" American civilization—an Atlantic civilization.[17] Whitman, Frank, and Mallea often coincide when meditating about the mission of the New World. Mallea also mentions Gertrude Stein,[18] Herman Melville,[19] Sherwood Anderson, T. S. Eliot, Henry James, Carl Sandburg, e. e. cummings, and Robert Louis Stevenson.

Professor Arnold Chapman has written an essay on Sherwood Anderson and Eduardo Mallea, finding similarities of spirit and form in them. Mallea has a great predilection for the author of *Winesburg, Ohio:*

As I write these lines, a man has died in Panama. He represented to the utmost degree the potential of the young soul of this our continent. He was Sherwood Anderson. His departure shocks me strangely, because ever since I've been working on this essay I have linked his name to my urgent need of formulating these still nebulous ideas in the most coherent form possible.[20]

Chapman adds the following commentary: "Evidently, Mallea, a man forever trying to find the highest aesthetic expression of Americanism, has found a kindred spirit in Sherwood Anderson."

Since the days of his adolescence Salvador Novo has been "flirting" with the poetic techniques of some North American poets. Jaime Torres Bodet tells us that in 1922 Novo offered him the Spanish translation of a poem by Edgar Lee Masters for *Falange,* a magazine published by Mr. Torres Bodet at the time. In the same issue, Rafael Lozano, discussing poetry in the United States, says that Masters wrote "a type of free verse" that he found "lacking in sonority." According to the editor of *Falange,* this type of free verse "was to be a most versatile instrument in the hands of Novo."

Xavier Villaurrutia always had a fondness for the Anglo-Saxon cultures. He translated some of Blake's works and became quite involved with the Little Theater movement. He even made a trip to Yale to study the technique of the theater. He began his book of poems, *Nostalgia de la muerte,* with a quotation from Michael Drayton: "Burned in a sea of ice, and drowned amidst fire. . . ." In it we find his "North Carolina Blues," which he dedicated to Langston Hughes. Even without the dedication this work would bring to mind the Negro poet.

The work of José Antonio Portuondo, the Cuban essayist, is typical of the keen interest in the literature of the United States felt by the young intellectuals of Spanish America. In two essays, entitled "The Expressionistic Passion of William Faulkner" and "William Faulkner and Southern Conscience," Portuondo discusses with insight and knowledge the subject matter and literary techniques of the North American writer. In his "Literary Process of Ernest Hemingway" he gives one of the best definitions I have seen of that striking novelist's art.[21] He is well acquainted with the most distinguished craftsmen in the American literary profession and has increased the Spanish-reading public's familiarity with such names as Gertrude Stein, Wallace Stevens, Ezra Pound, T. S. Eliot, e. e. cummings, and Scott Fitzgerald.

There is no avoiding the fact that North American literature has become popular in Hispanic America. In the nineteenth century only the works by well-known authors were translated. Writers like Poe and Longfellow were familiar to the readers of every country. Others attracted the attention of the more cultivated public. Besides those already mentioned, we find the names of Bryant, Melville, Emerson, Whittier, Whitman, Hawthorne, Jack London, Henry James, Harriet Beecher Stowe, Bret Harte, Irving, and O. Henry.

In this day and age there is hardly a North American writer who has not been translated into Spanish (even Mickey Spillane has made it) : Sherwood and Maxwell Anderson, Edith Wharton, Willa Cather, Stephen Crane, Thomas Wolfe, Pearl Buck, Eudora Welty, Katherine Anne Porter, Tennessee Williams, Richard Wright, William Carlos Williams, and many more. León Felipe, Ortíz de Montellano, and Rodolfo Usigli have shown especial predilection for T. S. Eliot and have rendered his work into Spanish.

In recent years Ezra Pound has been making headway in Spanish America. In 1956 José Vázquez Amaral translated his *Cantos,* and although he stated in his introduction that "poetry like this poetry cannot be translated," he gives us Cantos LXXIV to LXXXIV in Spanish—sprinkled with Latin, Greek, German, French, Italian, Provençal, and even Chinese words! There is also a smart edition of *Cinco Cantos,* translated by Margaret Bates, Violeta Gaudry Bancayan, E. L. Revol, and A. J. Weiss.[22]

In 1955, the Pan American Union published an anthology of contemporary North American poetry.[23] It is a bilingual edition with original and translation facing each other, and it covers the span between Edgar Lee Masters and Richard Wilbur. Some of the poets are rendered so well into Spanish that they seem to improve in the language of Cervantes. This is particularly true of "Yee Bow," the satiric yet "poetic" poem of Masters:

> They got me into the Sunday-school
> In Spoon River
> And tried to get me to drop Confucius for Jesus.
> I could have been no worse off
> If I had tried to get them to drop Jesus for Confucius.
> For, without any warning, as if it were a prank,
> And sneaking up behind me, Harry Wiley,
> The minister's son, caved my ribs into my lungs,
> With a blow of his fist.
> Now I shall never sleep with my ancestors in Pekin,
> And no children of mine shall worship at my grave.
>
> Me pusieron en la escuela dominical
> De Spoon River

Y trataron de que dejase a Confucio por Jesús.
No me hubiera ido peor
Si yo hubiese tratado de que ellos dejasen a Jesús por
    Confucio.
Porque sin avisarme y como en broma
Y sin dejar que yo lo viera, Harry Wiley,
El hijo del pastor, me hundió, de un puñetazo,
las costillas en los pulmones.
Y ahora no dormiré ya en Pekín con mis antepasados,
Y no tendré hijos que reverencien mi sepulcro.

The same statement is true also of the tender and, for all its objectivity, trembling poetry of William Carlos Williams:

TO WAKEN AN OLD LADY

Old age is
a flight of small
cheeping birds
skimming
bare trees
above a snow glaze.
Gaining and failing
they are buffeted
by a dark wind—
But what?
On harsh weedstalks
the flock has rested,
the snow
is covered with broken
seedhusks
and the wind tempered
by a shrill
piping of plenty.

La vejez es
un volar de
pajaritos que pían
y rozan
árboles desnudos,
sobre una cubierta de nieve.
Adelantan, se atrasan
combatidos
por un oscuro viento.
Pero ¿qué?
El bando ha descansado
en unas briznas duras de yerba
la nieve
se cubre de rotas
vainas de semillas
y el viento se templa
con un agudo
hervor de plenitud.

I have mentioned here only those American poets, novelists, and playwrights of great merit and established literary repute. There are, of course, the merely popular writers who cram the Spanish-American presses and tempt publishers with the hope of fast, easy money. (Unfortunately, they also lure many an innocent reader.) They are no credit to their fellow writers, and, as far as we are concerned, they merely corrupt the taste for literature that our schools and colleges try to cultivate in young spirits.

Spanish-American Novelists of Today

*D*URING the twenty years since my book *Novelistas contemporáneos de America*[1] was published many readers and literary critics have asked for an explanation of my methods of selection and my theory of criticism. A satisfactory answer would necessitate preparing an apologetic treatise on my ideas in this respect. Time and space do not permit me—on this occasion—to satisfy the request. Nevertheless, in a brief yet inclusive manner I shall give pertinent information that will make the reading of these and other pages of mine pleasurable and comprehension of them easy.

In the first volume of *Contemporary Novelists of America* there appear, among others, the names of Mariano Azuela, Rómulo Gallegos, Eduardo Barrios, Ricardo Guiraldes, José Eustasio Rivera, and Pedro Prado. My criterion for presenting these authors was chiefly the literary excellence of their novels and, to a lesser extent, the consensus of literary criticism about their value. The place these authors occupy in today's literary world amply shows the validity of my criterion.

I have always thought that the most precious gift of a critic is good literary taste. This is an intangible, subjective, and ineffable element, and solid documentation, a historical sense, erudite baggage, and so forth will never be able to substitute for good taste, despite the fact that they may be of inestimable value in critical labor. Good literary taste is much scarcer than culture and erudition, and for lack of it more than one great author has seen his value limited. The case of Marcelino Menéndez y Pelayo and his arbitrary judgments of Góngora and several Latin-American poets is an example.

Besides possessing good literary taste, it seems to me that the critic should express ideas and concepts with absolute simplicity. The critic simultaneously defines and orients; he is both philosopher and pedagogue. To envelop himself and the reader in a verbal hodgepodge, in a complicated nomenclature, which is almost always poorly translated from another language, is a capital sin of the new system of criticism. It is enough—it seems to me—that the novelist from Proust to Kafka, or the poet from Mallarmé to Jorge Guillén makes the process of communication difficult, but it is too much that the commentators on these artists follow the same process. I cite here the case of Amado Alonso and his explanation of Neruda's poems.

In order to facilitate study of the Spanish-American novel I have divided *Contemporary Novelists of America* into three parts, pertaining to novelists of the land, novelists of the city, and the modernist novelists. This classification did not seem adequate to a certain Peruvian critic, and in his study of the genre he made the following divisions: the novel as a general problem, the novel as an American expression, the colonial novel, the sentimental and idealistic novel, the psychological novel, the imaginative novel, the autobiographical novel, the *costumbrista* novel, naturalism, regional forms, the historical genre, war novels, the novel of adventures, the emigrant novel, anti-imperialist novels, the novel of the Mexican Revolution, the novel of the city, and the agrarian novel.

This classification is cumbersome and extremely incomplete. If the critic had waited a few more years, he would have had to include the novels of the revolutions of Guatemala, Costa Rica, Venezuela, Argentina, Colombia, Cuba, and many others. On the other hand, no novelist can be classified in a single category. My own classification serves merely for simplicity's sake. It is an elementary working tool, not a dogmatic and infallible formula.

Cedomil Goic has written an essay on the "Chilean Novel of Today."[2] During a forty-year period in Chilean literature, Mr. Goic speaks of superrealism, neorealism, *angurrientismo,* irrealism, the Biblical novel, and the scientific novel. If one were to apply this system of classification to the literatures of twenty countries for a period of one hundred years a great deal of confusion would arise and the perspective would be far too temporal. It might well be that in the small space occupied by a national literature these divisions would be more functional than in the vast panorama of continental literary production.

Permit me to sketch here a plan of today's Spanish-American novel, as an experiment or as a challenge. Let us not speak now of great novelists, but instead of representative novelists of America. My list would be composed of the following names: Miguel Ángel Asturias, Jorge Luis Borges, Alejo Carpentier, Carlos Fuentes, Jorge Icaza, Eduardo Mallea, Roa Bastos, Manuel Rojas, Juan Rulfo, and Agustín Yáñez. A book written about these novelists might be entitled "Personal History of the American Novel." The first inharmonious question would be: Why Asturias, Borges, Carpentier, Fuentes, Mallea, Roa Bastos, Rojas, Rulfo, and Yáñez? The second: Why not Spota, or Salarrué, or Caballero Calderón, or Aguilera Malta, or Marta Brunet, or Maria Luisa Bombal? Others would offer other names, other reasons, perhaps justifiable and pertinent. I shall try to explain my selection.

All of these novelists, besides being authors of depth, stand out as leaders of a generation. One might say that their novels synthesize the aesthetic and social tendencies of an era. All that defines a generation's countenance and content is found in the individual work— style, structural form, themes, the human condition, and the anguish of an era.

Miguel Ángel Asturias is a Guatemalan who possesses a knowledge of the vernacular language of his people as well as a high Spanish style. Originally a lyric poet of the vanguard, he later listened to the anguished cry of the oppressed masses of his nation, exploited by foreign enterprise. The novel serves him as an instrument of protest and redemption. Despite this, he does not abandon the poetic aspect of the novel, and he raises his theme of misery, poverty, suffering, and exploitation to an aesthetic plane. The vigorous social force of his works remains as a scaffolding for a structure of baroque combinations of rhythm, movement, angles, and perspective. The constant themes of his novels are political dictatorship (Estrada, Cabrera, Ubico, and others) and the abuses of the North American corporation, the United Fruit Company.

In his harsh novel, *Señor Presidente* (1946), Asturias offers us a picture of a nation subjected to the will of a brutal dictator. The novel has dramatic force, lyric fervor, and it reveals a profound love and knowledge of the people. Asturias' novel about the fruit company is cyclical. In several novels of the series he attacks the "Green God," with his seat in Wall Street, and in others, the subtle ways in which the company destroys all local competition. It is too bad that social realism has destroyed in this novelist the intimate critic of indigenous rites and mythology. At any rate, alongside the artist constantly goes the great fighter, so necessary in his country and in all of America.

Jorge Luis Borges is already a legend in Argentina.

Since Alfonso Reyes died, Borges has occupied the highest place in the intellectual life of the continent. His culture extends beyond the literary current and enters into the streams of history, social thought, and science. Possessing an eminent intelligence, he has fulfilled what Lugones tried to do and failed. He has delved into Oriental and Occidental literatures and has enriched his knowledge and imagination through them. He has mastered the language of the Gauchos, and he can express himself in the purest Spanish, with the ease of Garcilaso and the subtlety of Quevedo. He is not a novelist in the true sense of the word, yet his long stories contain so much material of high fiction that each continues to develop in the reader's mind. Borges bears strange similarities to Edgar Allan Poe; they share the concept of the mathematical development of the story, the sense of imminent tragedy, and the mysterious atmosphere of their stories. Poe, however, moves in a physical and temporal plane; Borges creates a unity of metaphysical time, and his characters, while perfectly logical, are abstract unities, fixations of ideas, specters from other worlds. Continuous concentration on the part of the reader is necessary to follow the interweaving of fancy, logic, and mystery. His sense of structural perfection is fulfilled in the brief novel, regardless of his chosen theme.

Alejo Carpentier is a great musicologist of Cuban-French nationality, the author of a book entitled *La música en Cuba,* as well as a fine writer of fiction. In *La música en Cuba* (1946), the magic of Afro-Cuban music has created a world of marvels, and this world has penetrated his world of fiction, making it rich in ancient legends and rituals. Magic realism ignites exotic visions, and the Negro—whether from Cuba or Haiti—attains extraordinary human and artistic dimensions in the work. *Los pasos perdidos* (1953) and *El reino de este mundo* (1949) demonstrate two aspects of his technique, with historical, ethical, picaresque, *costumbrista,* and folkloric ramifications.

In *El acoso* (1956) we witness the enormous nightmare of the pursued man, in his unavoidable march toward destruction—in the purely literary sense, a vision worthy of Poe or Kafka but, in the real sense, a typical Hispanic-American phenomenon. Elevating brutal reality to a plane of artistic creation is typical of this refined and transcendental author. That which in Lino Novás Calvo is direct violence and physical terror, or in Francisco Ayala a macabre caricature of fear, in Carpentier becomes an ingenious mechanism of artistic creation. Carpentier's style is luminous and musical, filled with tropical light, with the beat of barbarous hearts and with torments, subdued however by the discipline of his French genius.

Carlos Fuentes, the youngest of the Mexican novelists, has had great success with his well-named *La región más transparente* (1958). In the region of Mexico City, with its delicate splendor, the countryside and man are transparent. Fuentes' analysis of postrevolutionary Mexico and its society is truthful and cruel. As a sociological and psychological document *La región más transparente* is of lasting merit for its penetration and for the valor of the exposition. It is a pessimistic book, as are so many others dealing with the revolution. The importance of a novel of this type does not depend upon the success or failure of the matter discussed, but rather upon the author's vision and the technical and artistic means at his disposal.

Fuentes is a very gifted author. His novel reflects the confusion of Mexican society and the chaotic soul of the Mexican, whose conscious mind quivers in a world of continuous change while his subconscious is fixed in a profundity of myths and superstitions.

The entire vital experience of the Mexican is reduced to symbolic formulas. Racial forces compel him in one direction; his Aztec blood determines certain actions; but modern society—drenched with Yankee influence—drags him in still another direction. Fuentes observes these phenomena and manipulates his characters—capitalists, politicians, painters, and poets—serenely or foolishly, in salons of doubtful refinement, or during cocktail parties at which the blue-eyed damsel stands side by side with the dark-eyed Indian.

No one has examined more minutely and scathingly the human condition of the Ecuadoran Indian than Jorge Icaza, a strident novelist and the propagandist of a noble cause. His novel *Huasipungo* (1934) has gained him a great reputation in all of America—a just reputation considering Icaza's fervent sense of justice, but exaggerated from the viewpoint of the literary aspect of *Huasipungo*. In *Huasipungo* the enslaving power of telluric forces—transformed here into social and economic forces—overpowers the psychological development, destroying the man in order to give more relief to the doctrine. The dependence upon nature in novels such as *La vorágine, Doña Bárbara,* and *Os sertões* detracts from the man, reducing him to a pure accident. Moreover, in *Huasipungo* the Indian remains the prisoner of Marxist theory, without the possibility of individual will. For this reason, the characters in this novel are forgotten, and the reader's only recollection is that of an injustice, a violence, a violation of the elemental rights of man.

Human misery is a valid concern of fiction writers, and it can be elevated to a literary level. For this reason I attribute a great importance to Icaza's novels, but I consider his indifference to style and his use of a hybrid and prosaic language a great loss to Latin-American letters.

I do not believe that there is a great divergence of opinion regarding Eduardo Mallea. Of all Argentinian novelists he is most dedicated to examining the problems of his own destiny, the significance of his nation, and the human condition. Always the essayist, with his great and profound intelligence, he places himself in the tortured center of his novels. Mallea conceives of the novel as an interpretation, as a philosophical or sociological essay, or as an explanation of the formation of man, nations, and incipient cultures.

Several parallel themes result from his meditation: the hidden forces defining the character of his people; visible and invisible Argentina; the lack of communication among men as a constant reason for tragedy; and silence, immobility, and isolation as sources of creation.

It might be thought that a man as intellectual as Mallea would be restricted to a cold objectivism. Let us recall, however, that his first novel is entitled *Historia de una pasión argentina* (1937) and that in another, *Todo verdor perecerá,* human anguish acquires the characteristics of greatness. His work imparts a Socratic serenity—indicated by such titles as *Le ciudad junto al rio inmóvil* and *Bahía de Silencio*—but this is only one aspect of the author who at heart is both anguished and analytical. Meditation, analysis, passion, and intensity—all are qualities of Mallea, who furthermore is a very cultured man.

In order to observe the rapid advance in literary technique experienced in Argentina it would be useful to compare the work of Manuel Gálvez, which is realistic, documented, and prosaic, with the work of Mallea, which is philosophical, symbolic, and poetic. Gálvez' visible Argentina comes face to face with Mallea's invisible Argentina, reflected in a subterranean river that runs from the days of the struggle for independence to the present.

Roa Bastos' *Hijo de hombre* (1960) has just received an award in an Argentinian literary assembly. We have known that Roa Bastos was a surrealist, strongly influenced by Neruda, and one of the three best poets of Paraguay. With *Hijo de hombre* the poet acquires solid prestige as a novelist. *Hijo de hombre,* with its heroic acts, brutalities, and the pressure of cruelty and anguish suffered by the author, is a *tremendista* novel. We see not merely the episodes of the Chaco wars but their effect on man and his ideas. The work progresses from dramatic description to the formation of a revolutionary mentality. Roa Bastos fights to maintain the novel's independence from the dictatorship of external happenings, from the tyranny of the prevailing *ambiance,* from the invasion of destructive reality. In this sense it is in defense of mankind that Roa Bastos has avoided "realism" and created his characters in an ideal "other world." Just as *La región más trasparente* signals the most advanced point of the cyclical novel of the Mexican revolution, *Hijo de hombre* seems to determine the latest form of the Chaco war novel, the entrance of the genre into the region of universality, stripping it of a purely anecdotic aspect and limiting regionalism.

Manuel Rojas also fights for artistic liberation. Overcome by *criollismo,* the Chilean novel became a feigned *costumbrismo.* Just as artists of the *criollista* school painted cows that were excessively cowlike, authors introduced Gauchos that were excessively Gaucho-like. Manuel Rojas, since his very first stories, has interested himself more in man than in external forms of life, in man's anguish rather than in his social condition. Like a good poet, he has learned to write his novels with precision. The world of his experience is limited, and he repeats endlessly—from *El vaso de leche* (1935) to *Mejor que el vino* (1958), his autobiography in novel form. *Hijo de ladrón* is Rojas' best work, penetrating human anguish, describing it with exactness, and intensifying the game of social relationships. His most recent novel, *Punta de rieles,* is oriented toward questions of psychological analysis.

Manuel Rojas does not belong to any generation. Although he bears certain similarities to Gonzalez Vera, he is far from him in his aesthetic philosophy. A great sector of Chile is reflected in Rojas' novels, and their documentary significance assures him a permanent place in Chile's literary history.

The cult of Death occupies a luminous spot in Mexican mythology, and in modern times Death is considered merely the inverse of life. In Mexican painting, from Posada to Orozco and Montenegro, the skeleton is an omnipresent figure. Entire books have been written about the skull in Mexican art. Such vital artists as Diego Rivera and Alfaro Siqueiros maintain constant contact with Death. It should not surprise us then that an author like Juan Rulfo should choose a village of corpses as a setting for his novel, *Pedro Páramo* (1955).

By employing a peculiar concept of suspended time, *Pedro Páramo* forces the reader to lose his sense of reality and redeem a group of specters from Death. The reader becomes a part of this village from beyond the tomb and goes in search of Pedro Páramo in order to untangle the interrupted thread of his life. The reader learns many things that have gone on in the village.

The dead appear and live their life stories in a hermetic unity of eternal time created by the author.

If we think of Quevedo, the formula does not seem so original; nevertheless, the work of Juan Rulfo fuses time levels and conveys the author's absolute conviction that it is possible to pass immediately from one state to another. In order to succeed in such a daring literary enterprise great skill is needed; Rulfo possesses this domination of the forms of creation. He tackles reality in a symbolic manner, from the title of his novel to its conclusion, from the phantomlike sketch of his characters to his gray and dull use of adjectives.

Agustín Yáñez is the exact opposite of Juan Rulfo in several respects. He is a baroque stylist who allows himself to be carried away by his fiery imagination; but his mastery of literature—especially classical Spanish literature—enables him to control his verbal enthusiasm, and he subjects it to the most rigid laws of Castilian style. In his masterpiece, *Al filo del agua* (1955), Yáñez explores the hidden recesses of the national soul and explains the birth of music through the person of a young bell ringer.

He follows this youth in a second novel, *La creación,* tracing his studies in Europe, his great classical musical compositions, his return to popular Mexican music, and his ultimate ruin. Both fictitious and real people appear in the two novels—politicians, musicians, painters, poets, and actresses—with their real names or thinly veiled nicknames. The reader is left not knowing where fiction ends and reality begins in these frescoes filled with poetry, exaltation, tenderness, or tragedy—lyrical frescoes with the greatness of the murals of José Clemente Orozco or Diego Rivera.

The writers discussed in this chapter are—in my opinion—the outstanding novelists of Latin America. The brief discussions of each indicate the thematic wealth of the Latin-American novel.

Compared with the contemporary Spanish novel, the Latin-American novel is highly superior with regard to themes. The Spanish novelist—from Camilo José Cela to Juan Goytisolo, including Carmen Laforet, Ignacio Aldecoa, Ana María Matute, Sánchez Ferlosio, and Elena Quiroga—is unable to deal fully with the theme of man's circumstances. When an author disregards this he falls into a photographic method of description, which turns out to be a refuge in his political atmosphere. In Latin America one is able to write about dictatorship, and it has been done by all political novelists, from Mármol to Miguel Ángel Asturias. There is scarcely a *caudillo,* from Rosas to Ubico, who has not been the dramatic personage of some novel.

Alongside the theme of dictatorship goes that of the exploitation of the masses by foreign enterprise. At times this is purely economic exploitation, as in Cuba or Venezuela; at other times, it is complicated by racial oppression, in which case the protagonists of the tragedy are the Indians, abundant in the novels of Mexico, Peru, Guatemala, and Ecuador. Close to the theme of dictatorship is that of revolution and war. The Cuban revolution has already begun to produce its novelists, as the Mexican and Guatemalan revolutions and the wars of the Pacific and of the Chaco did before it.

Just as familiar as these matters of historical, economic, and social nature is the political novel that accuses and denounces. This is one of the richest veins of our literary mine. It appears with the first manifestations of socialism in the nineteenth century, and it has been intensified by today's Marxism. This tendency runs the same danger as that of demagogical propaganda, with the sorry loss of the pure elements of artistry. Many authors of merit have failed by attempting the hybridization of genres, and it is probable that Chilean literature has suffered more than any other in America from this fault.

The cruel analysis of society's vices is also typical of realism. We need only think of Blest Gana or of Orrego Luco. When a matter is studied with scientific scrupulosity and literary correctness as in the case of Fuentes' *La región más transparente* or Yáñez' *La creación*—the analysis becomes a literary category. (The present economic, moral, and cultural Chilean crisis offers all the necessary elements for this type of novel, and it is very strange that our young writers are bypassing such a wonderful opportunity, choosing instead to go on exotic and artificial pilgrimages.)

Just as the jungle, the plains, the Amazon, and the Andes annihilate man, the great Spanish-American city also becomes his enemy—the destroyer of his dreams, enthusiasm, tenderness, meditation, and repose.

The artist feels himself a stranger in a world of lowly interests, in which the rugged and brutal struggle for life sacrifices an individual's noble impulses, his desire for a spiritual life or for introspection. The modern city destroys first the poet and then the novelist. It gives him a false conception of his art, putting him in a competitive position. He must triumph with rhetorical fraud, with metaphors that become increasingly esoteric, and with disconcerting lyric motives. The novelist becomes a commentator on daily events, a facetious or pornographic fool, or an enemy of the established social order. The author becomes a choleric youth, a beatnik, an aspirant to a literary prize, a social figure, or a literary merchant. In all of these positions the novelist or the poet can easily become a comic or tragic figure, and as such he is incorporated into the world of fiction seen in the works of Carlos Fuentes, Agustín Yáñez, Eduardo Mallea, Gálvez, and Graciliano Ramos.

The great city isolates man, and, although he searches for understanding, his solitude drives him to despair. Communication is not always easy, and thus is born man's inner torture. As he searches in vain for a solution to the thousand inquietudes that assault him, he falls into a state of metaphysical torture. The novelist can look for his hero in this type of man, or in the woman who, filled with inexpressible ideals, moves uselessly in the shadows of her destructive silence. Her incapacity to communicate closes all doors of tenderness to her, and she engages in endless amorous calamities until her death.

The subconscious world preoccupies us, yet I do not believe that there are successful novels of this tendency in America. The surrealism possible in lyric poetry is not possible in novels. Only in the style called "magic realism" do we find traces of this Freudian influence.

I do not want to incur the error of Ortega y Gasset and predict the death of the *costumbrista* novel, or that of the *criollista* novel. On the contrary, I believe that *costumbrismo*—as a great factor in environment—is a permanent element in the realistic novel. *Criollismo* will disappear if the vital Creole world disappears; otherwise, it will endure, suffering the consequent transformation in the eternal game between reality and art. What might readily disappear is the Creole style, that is to say the transmutation of an incorrect and regressive language that in my opinion does not have the charm attributed to it by some.

I believe in the organic style of which Miguel de Unamuno speaks, but I believe even more in progress with respect to style. The better style corresponds to the higher culture. Rodó, Azorín, Rubén Darío, and Ortega learned to write well with study and effort. Mallarmé created his own style with the sweat of his brow; Jorge Guillén works at his poetic language with Benedictine devotion—day by day, minute by minute. Whoever has read the numerous editions of his *Cántico* knows what I am talking about.

For me there are not classical, romantic, or modernist styles. There are only good and bad styles. Thus,

Cervantes might be a romantic, Quevedo a modernist, and Rubén Darío a classicist. In Latin America, the writing style is generally poor, and many adherents of what is called the social novel believe that writing poorly is meritorious. Others believe that to write well is to invent a confusing style, loaded with technicalities and scientific terms, a habit of new critics throughout the world.

The spoken language of many Latin American countries—such as Chile, Cuba, and Argentina—tends toward degeneration. Strangely enough, this is happening in those countries of some of the most careful stylists, such as D'Halmar, Pedro Prado, María Luisa Bombal, Borges, Mallea, Martínez Estrada, and Alejo Carpentier. The writer knows that he has to protect his language, and if his influence is insignificant in the spoken language it must be all-powerful in written expression.

I am an incurable optimist in regard to questions of literary culture on our continent. I have tirelessly repeated in the United States that literature constitutes the strongest bond between the Americas, and that one can surely speak of literary Americanism, of a continental literary conscience. I have also said that the flower of our civilization is our literature, and the most viable blossoms have been produced by Andrés Bello, Sarmiento, Rodó, and Rubén Darío. Creative activity is so great that new names are added to the list of literary figures. New poets include Neruda, Vallejo, López Velarde, Nicolás Guillén, and Cecilia Merieles; new essayists, Portuondo, Mañach, Borges, and Picón Salas; and in addition to the novelists mentioned in this brief essay, there are the Brazilians Graciliano Ramos, Jorge Amado, José Lins do Rego, and Rachel de Queiroz. With Machado de Assís at their head, Brazilian writers have greatly contributed to development of the Latin American novel.

Some years ago, after studying the work of a His-panic-American thinker, I wrote the following:

Since colonial times the writers that have explained the spectacle of America and its inhabitants have come from out-side—"spectacle," because this and nothing more were the new lands for the discoverers and colonists, and they have continued to be a spectacle for the scientist of the eighteenth and nineteenth centuries and for the intellectual tourist of modern times. Since the days of Oviedo, to Keyserling, Seig-fried, and Frank, and including Darwin, Humboldt, and Prescott, only foreign voices have told us about our objective world, our spiritual horizon. We, through inertia, through the certainty of our inferiority, have been the guinea pigs—*cobaya aguti.* Proudly we have been this, with our hearts beating and our pupils ecstatic before the luminous glass of the microscope.[3]

We ourselves must tell the world our truth.

NOTES

HUMOR IN HISPANIC LITERATURE

[1] Also recommended is the J. M. Cohen translation, *The Adventures of Don Quixote* (Harmondsworth, Middlesex: Penguin Books, 1950).

[2] Alfonso Reyes, *Calendario* (Mexico City: Tezontle, 1945), p. 90.

[3] J. R. Spell, *The Life and Works of José Joaquín Fernández de Lizardi* (Philadelphia: University of Pennsylvania Press, 1931).

[4] Lewis Jacobs, "Charles Chaplin," in *Present Tense: The Arts of Living,* ed. Sharon Brown (New York: Harcourt, Brace and Co., 1941).

[5] Arturo Cancela, *Tres relatos porteños* (Buenos Aires: Gleizer, 1922).

JOSÉ ENRIQUE RODÓ AND HIS IDEALISTIC PHILOSOPHY

[1] José Enrique Rodó, *Ariel,* trans. F. J. Stimson (New York: Houghton Mifflin Co., 1922), p. 4; all quotations are from this edition.

[2] *Ibid.,* p. 15.
[3] *Ibid.,* p. 21.
[4] *Ibid.,* p. 25.
[5] *Ibid.,* p. 29.
[6] *Ibid.,* p. 31.
[7] *Ibid.,* p. 44.
[8] *Ibid.,* pp. 46–47.
[9] *Ibid.,* p. 50.
[10] *Ibid.,* pp. 64–65.
[11] *Ibid.,* p. 65.
[12] *Ibid.,* p. 70.
[13] *Ibid.,* pp. 71–72.
[14] *Ibid.,* p. 80.
[15] *Ibid.,* p. 81.
[16] *Ibid.,* p. 83.
[17] *Ibid.,* pp. 83–84.
[18] *Ibid.,* p. 84.
[19] *Ibid.,* p. 89.
[20] *Ibid.,* p. 101.
[21] *Ibid.,* p. 103.
[22] *Ibid.,* p. 104.
[23] *Ibid.,* p. 106.
[24] *Ibid.,* p. 110.
[25] *Ibid.,* p. 111.
[26] *Ibid.,* p. 112.
[27] *Ibid.,* p. 114.
[28] ***Ibid.***
[29] *Ibid.,* p. 119.
[30] *Ibid.,* p. 121.
[31] *Ibid.,* p. 122.
[32] *Ibid.,* p. 125.
[33] *Ibid.,* pp. 126–27.

[34] *Ibid.,* p. 129.

[35] *Ibid.,* p. 132.

[36] *Ibid.,* pp. 136–37.

[37] *Ibid.,* p. 142.

[38] *Ibid.,* p. 143.

[39] *Ibid.,* p. 144.

[40] Havelock Ellis, *The Motives of Proteus* (New York: Brentano's, 1928), p. xi.

[41] *Ibid.,* pp. xii, xiv.

SOME NOTES ON THE LITERARY INFLUENCE OF THE UNITED STATES IN SPANISH-AMERICAN LETTERS

[1] See Arturo Torres-Ríoseco, "Las teorías poéticas de Poe," *Ensayos sobre literatura latinoamericana* (Berkeley: University of California Press, 1953).

[2] V. J. Englekirk, *Edgar Allan Poe in Hispanic Literature* (New York: Instituto de las Españas, 1934).

[3] Mariano Latorre, "Bret Harte y el criollismo sudamericano," *Atenea,* XXXI, No. 123 (September, 1955), 437–62; and No. 124 (October, 1955), 105–39; quotation from p. 139.

[4] Pedro Henríquez Ureña, review of J. de L. Ferguson's *American Literature in Spain,* in *Revista de filogía española,* VII (1920), 62–71.

[5] *Ibid.,* p. 63.

[6] Balbío Dávalos, *Los grandes poetas norteamericanos* (Mexico: Tip. de la Oficina del Timbre, 1901).

[7] Rubén Darío, "Edgar Allan Poe," in *Los Raros* (Buenos Aires, 1896).

[8] Pedro Requena Legarreta (ed.), *Poetas muertos en la guerra* (Mexico City: Cultura, 1919).

[9] J. Fernández McGregor (trans.), Mark Twain's *Cuentos* (Mexico City, 1919).

[10] Pedro Henríquez Ureña, "Veinte años de literatura en los Estados Unidos," *Nosotros,* LVII (1927), 353–71.

[11] *Ibid.,* p. 353.

[12] Pedro Henríquez Ureña, *Literary Currents in Spanish America* (Cambridge, Mass.: Harvard University Press, 1945). José Antonio Ramos has carried on the work of Henríquez Ureña in a book entitled *Panorama de la literatura norteamericana* (Mexico City: Botas, 1935). In spite of his extensive reading and research, Ramos' work too closely follows the dictates of North American critics.

[13] Concha Zardoya, the Spanish writer, is the author of still another version, which has had wide circulation.

[14] Fernando Algería, *Walt Whitman en Hispano America* (Mexico City: Studium, 1954).

[15] Englekirk, *Edgar Allan Poe in Hispanic Literature.*

[16] Angel Flores, "Magical Realism in Spanish American Fiction," *Hispania,* XXXVIII (1955), 189.

[17] See Eduardo Mallea, *Meditación en la costa* (Buenos Aires: Imprenta Mercatali, 1939).

[18] See Eduardo Mallea, *Nocturno europeo* (Buenos Aires: Sur, 1935).

[19] See Eduardo Mallea, *Bahía de Silencio* and *Notas de un novelista* (Buenos Aires: Ed. Sudamericana, 1940).

[20] Quoted in Arnold Chapman, "Sherwood Anderson and Eduardo Mallea," *PMLA,* LXIX (1954), 34–45; 44.

[21] See José Antonio Portuondo, *El heroismo intelectual* (Mexico City: Tezontle, 1955).

[22] Preston H. Dittman (ed.), *Cinco cantos* (Miami, Fla.: Pandanus Press, 1952).

[23] *Antología de la poesia norteamericana contemporánea* (Washington, D.C.: Union Panamericana, 1955).

[1] Arturo Torres-Ríoseco, *Novelistas contemporáneos de América* (Santiago: Nascimento, 1940).

[2] Cedomil Goic, "La novela chilena actual," in *Estudios de lengua literatura como humanidades* (Santiago: Ed. Universitaria, s.a.).

[3] Arturo Torres-Ríoseco, "Introduction" to Humberto Palza, *El hombre como metodo* (San Francisco: Privately printed, 1939), pp. xi-xii.